1996 Supplement

CONSTITUTIONAL LAW

EDITORIAL ADVISORY BOARD
Little, Brown and Company
Law and Business Education

1996 Supplement

CONSTITUTIONAL LAW

Third Edition

Geoffrey R. Stone
Harry Kalven, Jr., Distinguished Service Professor of Law
and Provost
University of Chicago

Louis M. Seidman
Professor of Law
Georgetown University Law Center

Cass R. Sunstein
Karl N. Llewellyn Professor of Jurisprudence
University of Chicago Law School and
Department of Political Science

Mark V. Tushnet
Professor of Law
Georgetown University Law Center

Little, Brown and Company
Boston New York Toronto London

Library of Congress Catalog Card No. 90-63879

ISBN 0-316-81706-6

ICP

Published simultaneously in Canada
by Little, Brown & Company (Canada) Limited

PRINTED IN THE UNITED STATES OF AMERICA

Contents

Table of Cases

Italics indicate principal and intermediate cases.
All references are to page numbers in the main text.

Table of Authorities

Acknowledgments

Bezanson, Randall. Institutional Speech, 80 Iowa L. Rev. 735, 736, 755, 761, 739 (1995). Copyright © 1995 Iowa Law Review. Reprinted with permission.

Flaherty, Martin. The Most Dangerous Branch, 105 Yale Law Journal 1925, 1729-1730 (1996). Copyright © 1996 Yale Law Journal. Reprinted with permission.

Kagan, Private Speech, Public Purpose: The Role of Governmental Motive in First Amendment Doctrine, 63 U. Chi. L. Rev. 415, 467-475 (1996). Copyright © 1996 University of Chicago Law Review. Reprinted with permission.

Strauss, Affirmative Action and the Public Interest, 1995 Sup. Ct. Rev. 1, 3-4, 12-13. Copyright © 1996 University of Chicago Press. Reprinted with permission.

1996 Supplement

CONSTITUTIONAL LAW

Chapter One

The Role of the Supreme Court in the Constitutional Scheme

A. INTRODUCTION: SOME NOTES ON THE HISTORY AND THEORY OF THE CONSTITUTION

Page 22. At the end of section 4 of the Note, add the following:

See also Schacter, The Pursuit of "Popular Intent": Interpretive Dilemmas in Direct Democracy, 105 Yale L.J. 107 (1995), for an illuminating discussion.

E. "CASE OR CONTROVERSY" REQUIREMENTS AND THE PASSIVE VIRTUES

Page 121. At the end of the Note, add the following:

5. *Standing and voting rights.* What kind of injury must a plaintiff show to attack a districting scheme? Consider Shaw v. Hunt, 116 S. Ct. (1996) (infra this supplement), where the Court said simply,

> In United States v. Hays, 515 U.S. — (1995), we recognized that a plaintiff who resides in a district which is the subject of a racial-gerrymander claim has standing to challenge the legislation which created that district, but that a plaintiff from outside that district lacks standing absent specific evidence that he personally has been subjected to a racial classification. Two appellants, Ruth Shaw and Melvin Shimm, live in District 12 and thus have standing to challenge that part of Chapter 7 which defines District 12. The remaining appellants do not reside in District 1, however, and they have not provided specific evidence that they personally were assigned to their voting districts on the basis of race. Therefore, we conclude that only Shaw and Shimm have standing and only with respect to District 12.

Justice Stevens disagreed:

The Court's analysis of the standing question in this [reflects] the fact that the so-called *Shaw* claim [see text page 879, main volume] seeks to employ the federal courts to impose a particular form of electoral process, rather than to redress any racially discriminatory treatment that the electoral process has imposed. [I] begin by noting that this case reveals the Shaw claim to be useful less as a tool for protecting against racial discrimination than as a means by which state residents may second-guess legislative districting in federal court for partisan ends. The plaintiff-intervenors in this case are Republicans. It is apparent from the record that their real grievance is that they are represented in Congress by Democrats when they would prefer to be represented by members of their own party. They do not suggest that the racial identity of their representatives is a matter of concern, but it is obvious that their political identity is critical. [It] is plain that these intervenors are using their allegations of impermissibly race-based districting to achieve the same substantive result that their previous, less emotionally charged partisan gerrymandering challenge failed to secure.

[While] the plaintiffs purport to be challenging an unconstitutional racial gerrymander, they do not claim that they have been shut out of the electoral process on account of race, or that their voting power has been diluted as a consequence of race-based districting. What then is the wrong that these plaintiffs have suffered that entitles them to call upon a federal court for redress? In *Shaw I*, the majority construed the plaintiffs' claim to be that the Equal Protection Clause forbids race-based districting designed solely to "separate" voters by race, and that North Carolina's districting process violated the prohibition. Even if that were the claim before us, these plaintiffs should not have standing to bring it. The record shows that North Carolina's districting plan served to require these plaintiffs to share a district with voters of a different race. Thus, the injury that these plaintiffs have suffered, to the extent that there has been injury at all, stems from the integrative rather than the segregative effects of the State's redistricting plan.

Perhaps cognizant of this incongruity, counsel for plaintiffs asserted a rather more abstract objection to race-based districting at oral argument. He suggested that the plaintiffs objected to the use of race in the districting process not because of any adverse consequence that these plaintiffs, on account of their race, had suffered more than other persons, but rather because the State's failure to obey a constitutional command to legislate in a color-blind manner conveyed a message to voters across the State that "there are two black districts and ten white districts."

[To] be sure, as some commentators have noted, we have permitted generalized claims of harm resulting from State-sponsored messages to secure standing under the Establishment Clause. Pildes & Niemi, Expressive Harms, "Bizarre Districts," and Voting Rights: Evaluating Election-District Appearances After Shaw v. Reno, 92 Mich. L. Rev. 483, 499-524 (1993). It would be quite strange, however, to confer similarly broad standing under the Equal Protection Clause because that Clause protects against wrongs which by definition burden some persons but not others.

Here, of course, it appears that no individual has been burdened more than any other. The supposedly insidious messages that *Shaw I* contends will follow

> from extremely irregular race-based districting will presumably be received in equal measure by all State residents. For that reason, the claimed violation of a shared right to a color-blind districting process would not seem to implicate the Equal Protection Clause at all precisely because it rests neither on a challenge to the State's decision to distribute burdens and benefits unequally, nor on a claim that the State's formally equal treatment of its citizens in fact stamps persons of one race with a badge of inferiority in a context that results in no race-based, unequal treatment.

Consider also Justice Souter's dissenting opinion in Bush v. Vera, 116 S. Ct. — (1996) (infra Chapter V Section E, this supplement):

> Whereas malapportionment measurably reduces the influence of voters in more populous districts, and vote dilution predestines members of a racial minority to perpetual frustration as political losers, what *Shaw I* spoke of as harm is not confined to any identifiable class singled out for disadvantage. If, indeed, what *Shaw I* calls harm is identifiable at all in a practical sense, it would seem to play no favorites, but to fall on every citizen and every representative alike. The Court in *Shaw I* explained this conception of injury by saying that the forbidden use of race "reinforces the perception that members of the same racial group . . . think alike, share the same political interests, and will prefer the same candidates at the polls," and that it leads elected officials "to believe that their primary obligation is to represent only the members of that group, rather than their constituency as a whole." This injury is probably best understood as an "expressive harm," that is, one that "results from the idea or attitudes expressed through a governmental action, rather than from the more tangible or material consequences the action brings about." Pildes & Niemi, Expressive Harms, "Bizarre Districts," and Voting Rights: Evaluating Election-District Appearances after Shaw v. Reno, 92 Mich. L. Rev. 483, 506-507 (1993); see also id., at 493 ("The theory of voting rights [that *Shaw I*] endorses centers on the perceived legitimacy of structures of political representation, rather than on the distribution of actual political power between racial or political groups"). To the extent that racial considerations do express such notions, their shadows fall on majorities as well as minorities, whites as well as blacks, the politically dominant as well as the politically impotent.

What exactly is the injury involved in these cases? How, if at all, can the answer to that question be separated from an inquiry into the merits?

F. THE JURISDICTION OF THE SUPREME COURT

Page 146. At the end of Note 3, add the following:

4. *Not giving reasons.* In some of the areas we have discussed, the Court has, in a sense, declined to give reasons. When the Court denies certiorari, it does not explain itself. When the Court finds a case nonjusticiable, it may

do so partly because it does not want to address itself to the underlying issue. Frederick Schauer, in Giving Reasons, 47 Stan. L. Rev. 633 (1995), argues that reason-giving may have some of the problems associated with rules, and that it is sometimes legitimate not to give reasons. That is, reasons may be both over-inclusive and under-inclusive, and an institution that gives reasons may later have cause for regret. "When juries deliver verdicts, when the Supreme Court denies certiorari, when state supreme courts refuse review, when federal courts of appeals dispose of cases from the bench or without opinion, when trial judges rule on objections and frequently when they rule on motions, when lawyers exercise peremptory challenges and sometimes when judges dismiss jurors for cause, when housing and zoning authorities refuse to grant variances from their regulations, and sometimes when judges impose sentences, the conclusion stands alone, unsupported by reasons, justifications, or explanation." Can you think of factors that would justify a failure to give reasons? Might the answer lie partly in an assessment of the burdens of doing so and the likelihood that reasons will cause problems for the future?

Chapter Two

The Powers of Congress

A. INTRODUCTION

Page 149. At the end of the page, add the following:

For an overview of contemporary issues, see David L. Shapiro, Federalism: A Dialogue (1995).

Page 154. At the end of section 6 of the Note, add the following:

For an update on European developments, see Stephen Gardbaum, Rethinking Constitutional Federalism, 74 Tex. L. Rev. 795, 831-836 (1996).

B. THE BASIC ISSUES: FEDERALISM AND JUDICIAL REVIEW

Page 181. At the end of section 2 of the Note, add the following:

Consider these observations about why some matters ought to be left exclusively to state control: "[State] sovereignty over family law preserves the constitutional ideal of citizenship by promoting the development of civic virtue [in] maturing children. Federalism [destroys] the federal government's power to mold the moral character of future citizens in its own uniform image. [The] communitarian nature of family law requires a level of political engagement and a sense of community identity that lie beyond the reach of national politics. [As] the bonds of community thin out, the danger that shared values will degenerate into governmentally dictated values increases. By situating communitarian politics at the state level, [localism] ensures that the civic participation, political dialogue, and shared values essential to family law will develop within the states' smaller, relatively more accessible political locales. Second, state sovereignty over family law serves to diffuse governmental power over the formation of individual values and moral aspirations. [Localism] promotes diversity [in] the name of preserving citizen choice in matters of family life." Dailey, Federalism and Families, 143 U. Pa. L. Rev. 1787, 1820, 1871-1872 (1995). To what extent can a parallel argument be made as to education? Consumer protection laws?

Page 188. At the end of section 4 of the Note, add the following:

Consider this suggestion, from Regan, How to Think About the Federal Commerce Power and Incidentally Rewrite *United States v. Lopez*, 94 Mich. L. Rev. 554, 557, 560-561 (1995): "[In] thinking about whether the federal government has the power to do something or other, we should ask what special reason there is for the federal government to have that power. What reason is there to think the states are incapable or untrustworthy? [Is there] any reason why the regulation under consideration should come from the federal government[?]" Should this be supplemented by another question: "What reason is there to think that the courts are better able than Congress to determine whether the states are incapable or untrustworthy?"

D. THE NEW DEAL CRISIS AND THE RISE OF THE WELFARE STATE

Page 226. At the end of section 1 of the Note, add the following:

For a description of the background of *Jones & Laughlin*, see Casebeer, Aliquippa: The Company Town and Contested Power in the Construction of Law, 43 Buff. L. Rev. 617 (1995).

E. OTHER POWERS OF CONGRESS: ARE THEY MORE (OR LESS) PLENARY THAN THE COMMERCE POWER?

Page 251. After subsection 4b of the Note, add the following:

a. Baker, Conditional Federal Spending After *Lopez*, 95 Colum. L. Rev. 1911 (1995), criticizes the "political constraints" theory on the ground that it fails to deal with "the ability of *some states* to harness the federal lawmaking power to oppress *other states*." Conditional funding statutes, Baker argues, divide states into two groups, one of whose members "already willingly comply with, or favor, the stated condition." Representatives of such states may support a conditional funding statute to "garner the approval of 'single issue' voters and interest groups" or the votes of constituents who believe that activities in other state impose externalities on them. Id. at 1940-1943. Why is such action properly characterized as oppression?

F. IMPLIED LIMITS ON CONGRESS'S POWERS

Page 286. At the end of subsection 4 of the Note, add the following:

Consider these observations about the politics associated with unfunded mandates: "The nonaccountability explanation of unfunded mandates also presupposes that voters will discern the state and local tax and budgetary consequences of unfunded federal mandates less well than they discern the federal tax and budgetary consequences of federally funded regulation. [If] the nonaccountability explanation of unfunded mandates is correct, one would expect that state and local politicians would do everything in their power to reduce the cost to voters of gathering information about the connections between federal action and state and local finances." Dana, The Case for Unfunded Environmental Mandates, 69 S. Cal. L. Rev. 1, 18, 20 (1995).

Chapter Three

Judicial Efforts to Protect the Expansion of the Market against Assertions of Local Power

B. PROTECTION AGAINST DISCRIMINATION

Page 316. At the end of section 2 of the Note, add the following:

Heinzerling, The Commercial Constitution, 1996 Sup. Ct. Rev. 217, argues that the Court's unwillingness to assess the costs of outside commerce "on account of its outsider status" distorts its cost-benefit calculations. She argues that in-state residents believe that outside commerce imposes costs because it is "intrusive" and "forced" on the in-staters, and that these are as much costs of the outside commerce as the "statistical risk of physical harm" with which the Court's analysis is exclusively concerned: "'Dangerousness' and 'cost' do not [include] the qualitative attributes of risk."

Page 323. At the end of section 1 of the Note, add the following:

Consider this summary: Existing doctrine "create[s] the following modified process-reinforcing regime: When the costs of a potential state policy will be shared between an organized but out-of-state interest group and a diffuse group of local residents, the courts will presume that the diffuse locals will virtually represent the out-of-state interests against the policy when the policy requires an expenditure of tax dollars, but they will not so presume when the policy is implemented through regulation alone." Korobkin, The Local Politics of Acid Rain: Public Versus Private Decisionmaking and the Dormant Commerce Clause in a New Era of Environmental Law, 75 B.U. L. Rev. 689, 756 (1995). Why are the diffuse interests of taxpayers better able to represent out-of-state interests than the diffuse interests of consumers affected by higher prices due to regulation?

D. PREEMPTION

Page 383. As new subsection 4a of the Note, add the following:

4a. *Recent case*: Medtronic, Inc. v. Lohr, 116 S. Ct. — (1996), held that the federal statute establishing a process for allowing medical devices on to the market if they were substantially equivalent to devices marketed before 1976 did not preempt state tort causes of action for injuries due to negligent design, failure to comply with federal regulations, and negligent manufacturing and labelling. The federal statute's express preemption provision states: "[No] State [may] establish or continue in effect [any] requirement which is different from, or in addition to, any requirement applicable under this chapter to the device, and [which] relates to the safety or effectiveness of the device." Justice Breyer concurred in the result. Justice O'Connor, joined by Chief Justice Rehnquist and Justices Scalia and Thomas, dissented.

Chapter Four

The Distribution of National Powers

C. DOMESTIC AFFAIRS

Page 419. Before subsection 2b of the Note, add the following:

In Jones v. Clinton, 72 F.3d 1254 (8th Cir. 1996), the court of appeals reversed the district court insofar as that court had delayed the trial until the conclusion of the President's term.[1]

1. In the interests of disclosure, we note that one of the coauthors of this casebook represented President Clinton when he filed a petition for certiorari in this matter.

Page 425. Before the Note, add the following:

With regard to the formalist/functionalist debate, consider Flaherty, The Most Dangerous Branch, 105 Yale L.J. 1725, 1729-1730 (1996):

> The Founders embraced separation of powers to further several widely agreed-upon goals [including] balance among the branches, responsibility or accountability to the electorate, and energetic, efficient government. Currently, these goals are seen to be almost necessarily in tension, with balance cutting against a unitary presidency but accountability and energy cutting in its favor. The light shed by the Founding suggests that this need not be the case. On the one hand, an examination of the period only confirms the foundational importance of balance. In this light, the emergence of the administrative state renders congressional regulation of the executive branch more crucial than ever before, especially since Congress enjoyed extensive regulatory authority even when it was still the most dangerous branch. On the other hand, a better understanding of the Founding undermines current thinking about accountability and energy. Contrary to the usual scholarly assumptions [the] Founders sought to tame, not further empower, those divisions of government that claim a special responsiveness to the electorate. On this basis, the need for congressional regulation becomes imperative precisely because of the modern presidents' claim to electoral accountability. Conversely, many of the Founders did extol separation of powers as a way to accord government greater energy, much as modern constitutional

thinkers do today. Viewed in context, however, that commitment was modest, especially given the sheer scope of modern governmental activity.

These basic strategies—first, a faithful reconstruction of the doctrine's origins, and second, the attendant reconciliation of the purposes underlying separation of powers—confirm the [intuition] that there is something anomalous about the judiciary shielding what is now the most powerful office in the nation [i.e., the Presidency]. These approaches refute the idea that the Founders had developed a thoroughgoing, tripartite baseline capable of resolving modern controversies. They demonstrate that balance favors a flexible approach, that accountability bolsters this view, and that energy in the modern context is largely irrelevant. They point, finally, toward doctrinal bases for congressional regulation that are more thoroughgoing than anything currently mooted in separation of powers scholarship.

Page 428. After the first paragraph of section 3 of the Note, add the following:

For the Court's latest refusal to invoke the nondelegation doctrine, see Loving v. United States, 116 S. Ct. 1737 (1996). After a lower court invalidated the federal statute permitting courts martial to impose the death penalty, the President attempted to meet the constitutional objections to the statute by promulgating regulations requiring consideration of aggravating and mitigating factors before a death sentence was imposed. The underlying statutes provided that "[the] punishment which a court-martial may direct for an offense may not exceed such limits as the President may prescribe for that offense," and that a court martial "may, under such limitations as the President may prescribe, adjudge any punishment not forbidden by [the statute], including the penalty of death." Loving, who had been sentenced to death under the new procedure, argued that this statutory framework failed to establish an "intelligible principle" guiding the President's discretion and therefore had violated the nondelegation doctrine. Writing for the Court, Justice Kennedy rejected the argument:

> We think [that] the question to be asked is not whether there was any explicit principle telling the President how to select aggravating factors, but whether any such guidance was needed given the nature of the delegation and the officer who is to exercise the delegated authority. First, the delegation is set within boundaries the President may not exceed. Second, the delegation here was to the President in his role as Commander in Chief. Perhaps more explicit guidance as to how to select aggravating factors would be necessary if delegation were made to a newly created entity without independent authority in the area. [The] President's duties as Commander in Chief, however, require him to take responsible and continuing action to superintend the military, including the courts-martial.

Page 442. Before the Note, add the following:

The House of Representatives recently initiated a "Corrections Day" to deal with relatively uncontroversial measures correcting statutory gaps and mistakes made by drafters or by administrative agencies interpreting federal statutes. Under the new procedures, the Speaker has the authority to place bills on a special, expedited calendar, to be called twice per month. The bills are subject to only very limited amendment and require a three-fifths vote for passage. See H. Res. 168, 104th Cong, 1st Sess. (1995), quoted in 141 Cong. Rec. H6104 (daily ed. June 20, 1995). Consider the extent to which this procedure serves the function of the legislative veto. For a description and defense of "Corrections Day," see Nagle, Corrections Day, 43 UCLA L. Rev. 1267 (1996).

Page 453. Before section 3 of the Note, add the following:

In April of 1996, Congress passed and the President signed into law P.L. 104-130, 110 Stat. 1200. The Act utilizes procedures along the lines of the House bill described in the main text to grant the President a line item veto with respect to "appropriations, new direct spending, and limited tax benefits."

Page 454. Before section 4 of the Note, add the following:

3a. *Supermajority requirement for income tax increases.* On January 4, 1995, the House of Representatives implemented a provision in the "Contract with America" by adopting a rule requiring a three-fifths majority of those present and voting to pass an increase in income tax rates. See Rules of the House of Representatives Effective for the One Hundred Fourth Congress, House Rule XXI(5)(c). Is the rule unconstitutional? Consider Comment, An Open Letter to Congressman Gingrich, 104 Yale L.J. 1539, 1541 (1995):

> On seven different occasions, [the Constitution] stipulates a supermajority requirement. [But] it never places any special obstacles in the way of the enactment of ordinary legislation signed by the President. As the *Chadha* case teaches, this carefully considered lawmaking system can only be changed by constitutional amendment. . . .
>
> It is true that the Constitution gives each house the right "to determine the rules of its proceedings." This sensible housekeeping provision, however, does not authorize the House to violate fundamental principles of constitutional democracy. It simply authorizes the House to organize itself for informed and efficient debate and decision.

Compare McGinnis & Rappaport, The Constitutionality of Legislative Supermajority Requirements: A Defense, 105 Yale L.J. 483, 486, 492 (1995):

> [The Constitution does not specify] the proportion of a chamber necessary to pass a bill. Rather [it] simply [refers] to a bill's passage by a house or an order's receipt of the concurrence of a house. The Constitution's failure to specify a proportion necessary to pass a bill, combined with the delegation of authority to each house under the Rules of Proceedings Clause, suggests that the Constitution permits each house to decide how many members are necessary to pass a bill. . . .
>
> If the Constitution contained a majority-voting requirement for legislation, *Chadha* would, of course, support the conclusion that Congress could not depart from the requirement. But the question here is *whether* the Constitution contains such a requirement, and *Chadha* provides no guidance on this point.

Page 468. Before section 3 of the Note, add the following:

Consider Nourse, Toward a "Due Foundation" for Separation of Powers: The Federalist Papers as Political Narrative, 74 Tex. L. Rev. 447, 520 (1996):

> [The] Supreme Court was right to reject the removal argument in *Morrison*, albeit for the wrong reasons. If the separate exercise of power is our goal, then the independent counsel, like other independent agencies, poses little threat of structural collapse. By limiting the president's removal power, Congress does not gain, for itself, the ability to infiltrate the executive department. [Indeed,] it is ironic but true that the very idea of independence enshrined in the independent-counsel law replicates the underlying principles of *separation* of powers—the idea that independent persons achieve separate powers. If there is a problem with the independent counsel, it is not that it is not "separate" from other departments—it is that it is "too separate" from the people and thus raises important questions of accountability. Those questions are different in nature and kind, however, from questions about what separates the departments.

D. FOREIGN AFFAIRS

Page 477. At the end of the page, add the following:

Consider Sofaer, The Power over War, 50 Miami L. Rev. 33, 35-36 (1995):

> Congress clearly has the upper hand with regard to war, as it controls the means of warmaking, and can punish Presidents for disregarding its instructions. On the other hand, the President has substantial powers related to war that the Constitution enables the President to use independently. The President's powers over the conduct of foreign affairs, for example, can lead the nation into conflicts, and can even cause war. Similarly, the President's power as Commander in Chief encompasses the power to utilize the troops, ships, planes, and missiles supplied by Congress to defend the territory, armed forces, citizens, and commerce of the United States, even though such actions involve the use of force and can lead to broader conflict amounting to war.

> Nothing in the record of the Constitution's adoption justifies [the] view that the President's powers cannot be exercised if they involve use of force, until and unless Congress authorizes such action. [Neither] the decision to clog the road to combat, nor the determination to design a system that forces legislative review of war-related issues, establishes an intent to require the legislature to exercise the power conferred, to interfere with a decision by the President to use force, or to reach a conclusion on these issues in any respect.

Page 481. At the end of the page, add the following:

d. *United Nations "peacekeeping" and "peace enforcement."* In recent years, the President has authorized use of American forces in United Nations-sponsored military actions in Bosnia, Haiti, and Somalia. In each of these cases, the President did not seek prior congressional approval before troops were committed. Does the Constitution require congressional action before troops are sent as "peacekeepers" or "peace enforcers"? Consider Stromseth, Collective Force and Constitutional Responsibility: War Powers in the Post-Cold War Era, 50 Miami L. Rev. 145, 165, 166 (1995):

> [Given] the spectrum of U.N.-authorized military actions, the authority of the President to commit American forces without congressional approval will vary depending on the nature and risks of each operation. At one end of the spectrum are actions that clearly have the character and risks of "war" and are best understood as requiring prior authorization from Congress. At the other end of the spectrum are [peacekeeping] operations that enjoy the consent of all of the parties and are deployed in situations posing little risk of hostilities. Although Congress may limit American involvement in such peacekeeping operations, the President has a strong argument that sending American forces to these operations falls within well-established historical patterns of presidential peacetime troop deployments. Many if not most of the U.N.-authorized operations in which the United States is likely to participate, however, will fall into the more ambiguous middle ground. These include ["peace] enforcement" operations involving hostilities, but on a limited scale. Strong constitutional arguments in favor of congressional authorization can be made in many such cases, but grey areas and room for disagreement admittedly will exist.

For a comprehensive history of presidential warmaking, concluding that contemporary assertions of executive power "would have astonished the framers of the Constitution," see L. Fisher, Presidential War Power (1995).

Page 489. Before section 3 of the Note, add the following:

For a detailed analysis, see Raven-Hansen & Banks, From Vietnam to Desert Shield: The Commander in Chief's Spending Power, 81 Iowa L. Rev. 79 (1995).

Chapter Five

Equality and the Constitution

A. RACE AND THE CONSTITUTION

Page 558. After the quotation from "The Hollow Hope" in the middle of the page, add the following:

For representative criticism of Rosenberg's position, see Schultz & Gottlieb, Legal Functionalism and Social Change: A Reassessment of Rosenberg's The Hollow Hope: Can Courts Bring About Social Change?, 12 J.L. & Pol. 63 (1996). Schultz and Gottlieb argue that "[if] *Brown* had not occurred, other items, such as the Cold War or McCarthyism might have filled the [legislative] agenda. *Brown* put something on the agenda and made it acceptable and legitimate to criticize segregation. It was a necessary step in the process leading to desegregation, although not a sufficient one." Id. at 77.

B. EQUAL PROTECTION METHODOLOGY: RATIONAL BASIS REVIEW

Page 589. Before subsection 2b of the Note, add the following:

In Romer v. Evans, 116 S. Ct. 1620 (1996), the Court relied on *Moreno* to invalidate a Colorado constitutional amendment that prohibited local measures outlawing discrimination against homosexuals. The Court stated:

> Amendment 2 fails, indeed defies, [conventional rational basis] inquiry. First, the amendment has the peculiar property of imposing a broad and undifferentiated disability on a single named group, an exceptional and [invalid] form of legislation. Second, its sheer breadth is so discontinuous with the reasons offered for it that the amendment seems inexplicable by anything but animus toward the class that it affects; it lacks a rational relationship to legitimate state interests. . . .

> [Laws] of the kind now before us raise the inevitable inference that the disadvantage imposed is born of animosity toward the class of persons affected. "If the constitutional conception of 'equal protection of the laws' means anything, it must at the very least mean that a bare . . . desire to harm a politically unpopular group cannot constitute a legitimate governmental interest." [*Moreno*]. Even laws enacted for broad and ambitious purposes often can be explained by reference to legitimate public policies which justify the incidental disadvantages they impose on certain persons. Amendment 2, however, in making a general announcement that gays and lesbians shall not have any particular protections from the law, inflicts on them immediate, continuing, and real injuries that outrun and belie any legitimate justifications that may be claimed for it.

Compare Justice Scalia's dissenting opinion:

> The Court's opinion contains grim, disapproving hints that Coloradans have been guilty of "animus" or "animosity" toward homosexuality, as though that has been established as Unamerican. Of course it is our moral heritage that one should not hate any human being or class of human beings. But I had thought that one could consider certain conduct reprehensible—murder, for example, or polygamy, or cruelty to animals—and could exhibit even "animus" toward such conduct. Surely that is the only sort of "animus" at issue here: moral disapproval of homosexual conduct, the same sort of moral disapproval that produced the centuries-old criminal laws that we held constitutional in Bowers [v. Hardwick].

For a more detailed discussion of *Romer*, see this Supplement to page 780 of the main volume.

C. EQUAL PROTECTION METHODOLOGY: HEIGHTENED SCRUTINY AND THE PROBLEM OF RACE

Page 614. Before section 2 of the Note, add the following:

Compare Cole, The Paradox of Race and Crime: A Comment on Randall Kennedy's "Politics of Distinction," 83 Geo. L. Rev. 2547, 2551 (1995):

> The effect Kennedy has identified is attributable not to anything inherent in practices with a disparate impact, but rather to the phenomenon of intraracial crime. In this setting, anything the state does—intentional or not—that helps law-abiding African Americans is likely to burden law-violating African-Americans, and vice versa. Thus, Kennedy's argument would suggest that all discrimination in criminal law enforcement should be subject to minimal scrutiny.

Page 618. Before section 2 of the Note, add the following:

In United States v. Armstrong, 116 S. Ct. 1480 (1996), the Court held that, because a criminal defendant had failed to make the necessary threshold showing that the government had declined to prosecute similarly situated suspects of other races, he was not entitled to discovery from the government on a discriminatory prosecution claim. The defendant had been charged with conspiring to possess with intent to distribute "crack" cocaine. In support of his discovery motion, he offered an affidavit alleging that in every one of twenty-four similar cases closed by the Federal Public Defender Office during the year in question, the defendant was black. In addition, he submitted an affidavit from one of his attorneys alleging that an intake coordinator at a drug treatment center had told her that there were "an equal number of caucasian users and dealers to minority users and dealers," an affidavit from another criminal defense attorney alleging that in his experience many nonblacks were prosecuted in state court for crack offenses, and a newspaper article reporting that federal "crack criminals . . . are being punished far more severely than if they had been caught with powder cocaine, and almost every single one of them is black." The district court granted the defense request, and the court of appeals affirmed. In an 8-1 decision, the Court, per Chief Justice Rehnquist, reversed. The Court held that

> To establish a discriminatory effect in a race case, the claimant must show that similarly situated individuals of a different race were not prosecuted. . . .
>
> [If] the claim of selective prosecution were well founded, it should not have been an insuperable task to prove that persons of other races were being treated differently than respondents. [We] think the required threshold—a credible showing of different treatment of similarly situated persons—adequately balances the Government's interest in vigorous prosecution and the defendant's interest in avoiding selective prosecution. . . .
>
> The Court of Appeals reached its decision in part because it started "with the presumption that people of *all* races commit *all* types of crimes—not with the premise that any type of crime is the exclusive province of any particular racial or ethnic group." It cited no authority for this proposition, which seems contradicted by the most recent statistics of the United States Sentencing Commission. Those statistics show that: More than 90% of the persons sentenced in 1994 for crack cocaine trafficking were black; 93.4% of convicted LSD dealers were white; and 91% of those convicted for pornography or prostitution were white. Presumptions at war with presumably reliable statistics have no proper place in the analysis of this issue.

The Court found the defendant's study inadequate because it "failed to identify individuals who were not black, could have been prosecuted for the offenses for which respondents were charged, but were not so prosecuted." It dismissed the newspaper article as irrelevant to the allegation of discrimination in prosecutorial decisions and the other affidavits as "hearsay" and "personal conclusions based on anecdotal evidence." It distinguished *Batson* as follows:

> During jury selection, the entire *res gestae* take place in front of the trial judge. Because the judge has before him the entire venire, he is well situated to detect whether a challenge to the seating of one juror is part of a "pattern" of singling out members of a single race for peremptory challenges. He is in a position to discern whether a challenge to a black juror has evidentiary significance; the significance may differ if the venire consists mostly of blacks or of whites. Similarly, if the defendant makes out a prima facie case, the prosecutor is called upon to justify only decisions made in the very case then before the court. The trial judge need not review prosecutorial conduct in relation to other venires in other cases.

Only Justice Stevens dissented:

> The Court correctly concludes that in this case the facts presented to the District Court in support of respondents' claim that they had been singled out for prosecution because of their race were not sufficient to prove the defense. [I] am persuaded[, however,] that the District Judge did not abuse her discretion when she concluded that the factual showing was sufficiently disturbing to require some response from the United States Attorney's Office.

Note that the defendant did not allege that the statutory penalties for possession and distribution of "crack" were influenced by the racial composition of the class charged with violating the statute. How should such a claim be evaluated? In *Batson* and other cases, the Court has stated that the constitutional prohibition against race discrimination prevents the state from relying on even accurate racial generalizations. Does Chief Justice Rehnquist violate this norm when he relies on the supposedly different propensities of racial groups to commit different crimes?

Page 635. At the end of section 2, add the following:

In Bush v. Vera, 116 S. Ct. — (1996), a plurality of the Court held that although the shape of the district was only of evidentiary significance when the issue was the triggering of heightened scrutiny, it bore directly on whether there was the "narrow tailoring" that heightened scrutiny requires:

> Our discussion in *Miller* served only to emphasize that the ultimate constitutional values at stake involve the harms caused by the use of unjustified racial classifications, and that bizarreness is not necessary to trigger strict scrutiny. Significant deviations from traditional districting principles, such as the bizarre shape and noncompactness demonstrated by the districts here, cause constitutional harm insofar as they convey the message that political identity is, or should be, predominantly racial. For example, the bizarre shaping of Districts 18 and 29, cutting across pre-existing precinct lines and other natural or traditional divisions, is not merely evidentially significant; it is part of the constitutional problem insofar as it disrupts nonracial bases of political identity and thus intensifies emphasis on race.

Bush is discussed in greater detail in Chapter 6 Section E of this Supplement.

Page 648. At the end of section 4 of the Note, add the following:

In Romer v. Evans, 116 S. Ct. 1620 (1996), the Court utilized rational basis review to invalidate an amendment to the Colorado constitution that prohibited localities from enacting laws that protected homosexuals from discrimination. The Court stated:

> It is not within our constitutional tradition to enact laws of this sort. Central both to the idea of the rule of law and to our own Constitution's guarantee of equal protection is the principle that government and each of its parts remain open on impartial terms to all who seek its assistance. "'Equal protection of the laws is not achieved through indiscriminate imposition of inequalities.'" Sweatt v. Painter (quoting Shelley v. Kraemer). Respect for this principle explains why laws singling out a certain class of citizens for disfavored legal status or general hardships are rare. A law declaring that in general it shall be more difficult for one group of citizens than for all others to seek aid from the government is itself a denial of equal protection of the laws in the most literal sense. "The guaranty of 'equal protection of the laws is a pledge of the protection of equal laws.'" Skinner v. Oklahoma ex rel. Williamson, (quoting Yick Wo v. Hopkins).

Compare Justice Scalia's dissent:

> The central thesis of the Court's reasoning is that any group is denied equal protection when, to obtain advantage (or, presumably, to avoid disadvantage), it must have recourse to a more general and hence more difficult level of political decisionmaking than others. The world has never heard of such a principle, which is why the Court's opinion is so long on emotive utterance and so short on relevant legal citation. And it seems to me most unlikely that any multilevel democracy can function under such a principle. For whenever a disadvantage is imposed, or conferral of a benefit is prohibited, at one of the higher levels of democratic decisionmaking (i.e., by the state legislature rather than local government, or by the people at large in the state constitution rather than the legislature), the affected group has (under this theory) been denied equal protection. To take the simplest of examples, consider a state law prohibiting the award of municipal contracts to relatives of mayors or city councilmen. Once such a law is passed, the group composed of such relatives must, in order to get the benefit of city contracts, persuade the state legislature—unlike all other citizens, who need only persuade the municipality. It is ridiculous to consider this a denial of equal protection, which is why the Court's theory is unheard-of.

For a more detailed discussion of *Romer*, see this Supplement to page 780 of the main volume.

Page 688. At the end of subsection e of the Note, add the following:

In connection with the political process argument, consider Strauss, Affirmative Action and the Public Interest, 1995 Sup. Ct. Rev. 1, 12-13:

In general, the notion of "consistency" used in *Adarand* and *Croson* would lead to implausible, even bizarre, conclusions. . . .

The Court has never ruled, for example, that homosexuals are a suspect class. Today, therefore, affirmative action legislation favoring homosexuals would be treated the same as legislation favoring, say, optometrists or any other group: all such legislation is almost automatically constitutional under the rational basis standard. But suppose the Court were to decide that the extent of prejudice against homosexuals is sufficiently great, and their political power sufficiently limited, to warrant declaring homosexuality a suspect classification. Under *Adarand* and *Croson*, that decision would automatically make it much more difficult to enact legislation favoring homosexuals than to favor optometrists or tobacco farmers. In other words, under the "consistency" principle, the decision that homosexuals have historically been discriminated against, are currently the victims of prejudice, and lack political power would yield the conclusion that legislation seeking to *aid* homosexuals is subject to strict scrutiny and generally unconstitutional. This cannot possibly be the right approach.

Page 692. At the end of the page, add the following:

Consider Addis, Role Models and the Politics of Recognition, 144 U. Pa. L. Rev. 1377, 1442-1443 (1996):

> Ironically, while the Supreme Court rejected the role model theory as an "amorphous" remedial measure in one context, it considered the notion sufficiently precise to justify exclusion and discrimination in another context. Thus, in Ambach v. Norwick, [441 U.S. 68 (1979)], the Supreme Court upheld a New York statute that permitted only United States citizens or persons who intended to apply for citizenship to receive a public school teaching certificate on the ground that "a teacher serves as a role model for his students, exerting a subtle but important influence over their perceptions and values." Justice Powell, the same Justice who, in *Wygant*, deemed the role model theory too ambiguous to justify race-based decisionmaking, seemed quite confident that the notion was precise enough to justify the state's exclusion of resident aliens from the teaching profession and to prevent that exclusion from violating the Equal Protection Clause of the Fourteenth Amendment.

d. *The public interest.* Can strict scrutiny for affirmative action measures be justified on the ground that it is designed to insure that such measures are really in the "public interest" rather than simply a part of a "racial spoils system"? Consider Strauss, Affirmative Action and the Public Interest, 1995 Sup. Ct. Rev. 1, 3-4:

> [What] the Court has done is to revive, in the area of affirmative action, one of the noble dreams of American public law—that courts should try to ensure that legislation does not just benefit narrow interest groups but instead serves a public interest. This dream has at times turned into what would generally be thought a nightmare, as in the *Lochner* era. The Court's selectivity, in dealing

only with affirmative action laws (and perhaps a few others) in this way, is hard to defend. There are enormous theoretical and practical problems in trying to define a public interest, as distinguished from special interests. But however questionable, the Court's approach to affirmative action should be understood and evaluated, as the latest display of this undeniably attractive leitmotif of American law.

Page 694. At the end of section 3 of the Note, add the following:

In Bush v. Vera, 116 S. Ct. — (1996), a three-Justice plurality of the Court assumed, without deciding, that compliance with section 2 of the Voting Rights Act was a compelling state interest justifying using race as a predominant factor in drawing district lines. Section 2 goes beyond prohibiting discriminatory intent in districting by imposing a "results" test: districts are illegal when protected groups "have less opportunity than other members of the electorate to [elect] representatives of their choice." The plurality nonetheless held that the districts in question were unconstitutional because they were "bizarrely shaped" and "far from compact" and because section 2 as previously interpreted by the Court did not "require race-based creation of a district that is far from compact." The plurality noted, however, that

> [i]f the State has a "strong basis in evidence" for concluding that creation of a majority-minority district is reasonably necessary to comply with §2, and the districting that is based on race "substantially addresses the §2 violation," it satisfies strict scrutiny. . . . A §2 district that is *reasonably* compact and regular, taking into account traditional districting principles such as maintaining communities of interest and traditional boundaries, may pass strict scrutiny without having to defeat rival compact districts designed by plaintiffs' experts in endless "beauty contests." [Under] our cases, the States retain a flexibility that federal courts enforcing §2 lack [insofar] as deference is due to their reasonable fears of, and to their reasonable efforts to avoid, §2 liability.

In an unusual concurrence to her own plurality opinion, Justice O'Connor wrote that in her judgment, compliance with the "results" requirement of section 2 was a compelling state interest. In a separate concurrence, Justice Thomas, joined by Justice Scalia, "[assumed] without deciding" that the State had asserted a compelling state interest. "Given that assumption, I agree that the State's redistricting attempts were not narrowly tailored to achieve its asserted interest." Justice Stevens, joined by Justices Ginsburg and Breyer, and Justice Souter, also joined by Justices Ginsburg and Breyer, filed dissenting opinions.

In Shaw v. Hunt, 116 S. Ct. — (1996), decided on the same day as *Bush*, the Court, in a 5-4 decision written by Chief Justice Rehnquist,

> [assumed] *arguendo* for the purpose of resolving this case, that compliance with §2 could be a compelling interest, and we likewise assume, *arguendo,* that the General Assembly believed a second majority-minority district was needed in order not to violate §2, and that the legislature at the time it acted had a strong basis in evidence to support that conclusion.

The Court nonetheless found the district unconstitutional because it was not narrowly tailored to meet the asserted end. This was so because a district that was not "narrowly compact" would not avoid a section 2 violation.

> If a §2 violation is proven for a particular area, it flows from the fact that individuals in this area "have less opportunity than other members of the electorate to participate in the political process and elect representatives of their choice" [quoting from section 2]. The vote dilution injuries suffered by these persons are not remedied by creating a safe majority-black district somewhere else in the State. For example, if a geographically compact, cohesive minority poulation lives in south-central to southeastern North Carolina, . . . [a district] which spans the Piedmont Crescent would not address that §2 violation. The black voters of the south-central to southeastern region would still be suffering precisely the same injury that they suffered before [the district] was drawn.

Bush and Shaw v. Hunt are discussed in more detail in this Supplement to Chapter 6 Section E of the main volume.

Page 696. Before section 6 of the Note, add the following:

For the Court's latest holdings regarding race-based congressional districting, see Shaw v. Hunt, 116 S. Ct. — (1996) and Bush v. Vera, 116 S. Ct. — (1996), discussed in Chapter 6 Section E of this Supplement to the main volume.

Consider Spann, Affirmative Action and Discrimination, 39 How. L. Rev. 1, 72 (1995):

> [The] consequence of *Adarand* will necessarily be to divert some societal resources from racial minorities to whites. The racial minorities who would have received societal resources under an affirmative action program that *Adarand* invalidates will no longer receive them; they will instead go to members of the white majority.
>
> This diversion of resources [is] good, old-fashioned racial discrimination, pure and simple. It disadvantages racial minorities to advance the interests of whites. It does so through the use of an explicit racial classification that distinguishes affirmative action programs from other resource allocation programs. It is the product of an official government body taking an official government action, with full knowledge of the adverse impact that its action will have on the interests of racial minorities. It inflicts a type of harm on racial minorities that, by

design and effect, is both widespread and pervasive. And it ultimately stigmatizes racial minorities in a way that brands them as inferior to whites.

D. EQUAL PROTECTION METHODOLOGY: HEIGHTENED SCRUTINY AND THE PROBLEM OF GENDER

Page 713. Before section 4 of the Note, add the following:

UNITED STATES v. VIRGINIA

116 S. Ct. — (1996)

JUSTICE GINSBURG delivered the opinion of the Court.

Virginia's public institutions of higher learning include an incomparable military college, Virginia Military Institute (VMI). The United States maintains that the Constitution's equal protection guarantee precludes Virginia from reserving exclusively to men the unique educational opportunities VMI affords. We agree.

I

Founded in 1839, VMI is today the sole single-sex school among Virginia's 15 public institutions of higher learning. VMI's distinctive mission is to produce "citizen-soldiers," men prepared for leadership in civilian life and in military service. VMI pursues this mission through pervasive training of a kind not available anywhere else in Virginia. Assigning prime place to character development, VMI uses an "adversative method" modeled on English public schools and once characteristic of military instruction. VMI constantly endeavors to instill physical and mental discipline in its cadets and impart to them a strong moral code. The school's graduates leave VMI with heightened comprehension of their capacity to deal with duress and stress, and a large sense of accomplishment for completing the hazardous course.

VMI has notably succeeded in its mission to produce leaders; among its alumni are military generals, Members of Congress, and business executives. The school's alumni overwhelmingly perceive that their VMI training helped them to realize their personal goals. VMI's endowment reflects the loyalty of its graduates; VMI has the largest per-student endowment of all undergraduate institutions in the Nation.

Neither the goal of producing citizen-soldiers nor VMI's implementing methodology is inherently unsuitable to women. And the school's impressive record in producing leaders has made admission desirable to some women. Nevertheless, Virginia has elected to preserve exclusively for men the advantages and opportunities a VMI education affords. . . .

II

A . . .

VMI produces its "citizen-soldiers" through "an adversative, or doubting, model of education" which features "physical rigor, mental stress, absolute equality of treatment, absence of privacy, minute regulation of behavior, and indoctrination in desirable values.". . .

VMI cadets live in spartan barracks where surveillance is constant and privacy nonexistent; they wear uniforms, eat together in the mess hall, and regularly participate in drills. Entering students are incessantly exposed to the rat line, "an extreme form of the adversative model," comparable in intensity to Marine Corps boot camp. Tormenting and punishing, the rat line bonds new cadets to their fellow sufferers and, when they have completed the 7-month experience, to their former tormentors.

VMI's "adversative model" is further characterized by a hierarchical "class system" of privileges and responsibilities, a "dyke system" for assigning a senior class mentor to each entering class "rat," and a stringently enforced "honor code," which prescribes that a cadet "'does not lie, cheat, steal nor tolerate those who do.'"

VMI attracts some applicants because of its reputation as an extraordinarily challenging military school, and "because its alumni are exceptionally close to the school." "Women have no opportunity anywhere to gain the benefits of [the system of education at VMI]."

B

[In 1990, the United States sued Virginia and VMI, alleging that VMI's admission policy violated the Equal Protection Clause. At the conclusion of a trial, the District Court found that "some women, at least" would want to attend VMI and were capable of all the activities required of VMI cadets. The district court nonetheless ruled in favor of VMI. The court acknowledged that women were denied a unique education opportunity available only at VMI, but held that if women were admitted "some aspects of the [school's] distinctive method would be altered." Specifically, allowance for personal privacy would have to be made, physical education requirements would have to be altered, and the adversative environment could not survive unmodified. The court found that these changes would impinge upon the state interest in diversity in public education.

[The Court of Appeals reversed, holding that "neither the goal of producing citizen soldiers nor VMI's implementing methodology is inherently unsuitable to women." It remanded the case to the district court for purposes of selecting a remedy.]

C

In response to the Fourth Circuit's ruling, Virginia proposed a parallel program for women: Virginia Women's Institute for Leadership (VWIL). The 4-year, state-sponsored undergraduate program would be located at Mary Baldwin College, a private liberal arts school for women, and would be open, initially, to about 25 to 30 students. Although VWIL would share VMI's mission—to produce "citizen-soldiers"—the VWIL program would differ, as does Mary Baldwin College, from VMI in academic offerings, methods of education, and financial resources.

The average combined SAT score of entrants at Mary Baldwin is about 100 points lower than the score for VMI freshmen. Mary Baldwin's faculty holds "significantly fewer Ph.D.'s than the faculty at VMI," and receives significantly lower salaries, While VMI offers degrees in liberal arts, the sciences, and engineering, Mary Baldwin, at the time of trial, offered only bachelor of arts degrees. A VWIL student seeking to earn an engineering degree could gain one, without public support, by attending Washington University in St. Louis, Missouri, for two years, paying the required private tuition.

Experts in educating women at the college level composed the Task Force charged with designing the VWIL program; Task Force members were drawn from Mary Baldwin's own faculty and staff. Training its attention on methods of instruction appropriate for "most women," the Task Force determined that a military model would be "wholly inappropriate" for VWIL. . . .

In lieu of VMI's adversative method, the VWIL Task Force favored "a cooperative method which reinforces self-esteem." In addition to the standard bachelor of arts program offered at Mary Baldwin, VWIL students would take courses in leadership, complete an off-campus leadership externship, participate in community service projects, and assist in arranging a speaker series.

Virginia represented that it will provide equal financial support for in-state VWIL students and VMI cadets, and the VMI Foundation agreed to supply a $5.4625 million endowment for the VWIL program, Mary Baldwin's own endowment is about $19 million; VMI's is $131 million. Mary Baldwin will add $35 million to its endowment based on future commitments; VMI will add $220 million. The VMI Alumni Association has developed a network of employers interested in hiring VMI graduates. The Association has agreed to open its network to VWIL graduates, but those graduates will not have the advantage afforded by a VMI degree.

D

[The district court approved this remedial plan, and the court of appeals affirmed.]

III

The cross-petitions in this case present two ultimate issues. First, does Virginia's exclusion of women from the educational opportunities provided by VMI—extraordinary opportunities for military training and civilian leadership development—deny to women "capable of all of the individual activities required of VMI cadets," the equal protection of the laws guaranteed by the Fourteenth Amendment? Second, if VMI's "unique" situation,—as Virginia's sole single-sex public institution of higher education—offends the Constitution's equal protection principle, what is the remedial requirement?

IV

We note, once again, the core instruction of this Court's pathmarking decisions in J. E. B. v. Alabama ex rel. T. B. [page 726 of the main volume] and *Mississippi Univ. for Women*: Parties who seek to defend gender-based government action must demonstrate an "exceedingly persuasive justification" for that action. . . .

Since *Reed*, the Court has repeatedly recognized that neither federal nor state government acts compatibly with the equal protection principle when a law or official policy denies to women, simply because they are women, full citizenship stature—equal opportunity to aspire, achieve, participate in and contribute to society based on their individual talents and capacities.

Without equating gender classifications, for all purposes, to classifications based on race or national origin,[6] the Court, in post-*Reed* decisions, has carefully inspected official action that closes a door or denies opportunity to women (or to men). To summarize the Court's current directions for cases of official classification based on gender: Focusing on the differential treatment or denial of opportunity for which relief is sought, the reviewing court must determine whether the proffered justification is "exceedingly persuasive." The burden of justification is demanding and it rests entirely on the State. The State must show "at least that the [challenged] classification serves 'important governmental objectives and that the discriminatory means employed' are 'substantially related to the achievement of those objectives.'" The justification must be genuine, not hypothesized or invented post hoc in response to litigation. And it must not rely on overbroad generalizations about the different talents, capacities, or preferences of males and females.

6. The Court has thus far reserved most stringent judicial scrutiny for classifications based on race or national origin, but last Term observed that strict scrutiny of such classifications is not inevitably "fatal in fact." [Adarand]

The heightened review standard our precedent establishes does not make sex a proscribed classification. Supposed "inherent differences" are no longer accepted as a ground for race or national origin classifications. See Loving v. Virginia. Physical differences between men and women, however, are enduring. . . .

"Inherent differences" between men and women, we have come to appreciate, remain cause for celebration, but not for denigration of the members of either sex or for artificial constraints on an individual's opportunity. Sex classifications may be used to compensate women "for particular economic disabilities [they have] suffered," to "promote equal employment opportunity," to advance full development of the talent and capacities of our Nation's people.[7] But such classifications may not be used, as they once were, to create or perpetuate the legal, social, and economic inferiority of women.

Measuring the record in this case against the review standard just described, we conclude that Virginia has shown no "exceedingly persuasive justification" for excluding all women from the citizen-soldier training afforded by VMI. We therefore affirm the Fourth Circuit's initial judgment, which held that Virginia had violated the Fourteenth Amendment's Equal Protection Clause. Because the remedy proffered by Virginia—the Mary Baldwin VWIL program—does not cure the constitutional violation, i.e., it does not provide equal opportunity, we reverse the Fourth Circuit's final judgment in this case.

V

[Virginia] asserts two justifications in defense of VMI's exclusion of women. First, the Commonwealth contends, "single-sex education provides important educational benefits," and the option of single-sex education contributes to "diversity in educational approaches." Second, the Commonwealth argues, "the unique VMI method of character development and leadership training," the school's adversative approach, would have to be modified were VMI to admit women. We consider these two justifications in turn.

7. Several amici have urged that diversity in educational opportunities is an altogether appropriate governmental pursuit and that single-sex schools can contribute importantly to such diversity. Indeed, it is the mission of some single-sex schools "to dissipate, rather than perpetuate, traditional gender classifications." We do not question the State's prerogative evenhandedly to support diverse educational opportunities. We address specifically and only an educational opportunity recognized by the District Court and the Court of Appeals as "unique," an opportunity available only at Virginia's premier military institute, the State's sole single-sex public university or college.

A

Single-sex education affords pedagogical benefits to at least some students, Virginia emphasizes, and that reality is uncontested in this litigation. Similarly, it is not disputed that diversity among public educational institutions can serve the public good. But Virginia has not shown that VMI was established, or has been maintained, with a view to diversifying, by its categorical exclusion of women, educational opportunities within the State. In cases of this genre, our precedent instructs that "benign" justifications proffered in defense of categorical exclusions will not be accepted automatically; a tenable justification must describe actual state purposes, not rationalizations for actions in fact differently grounded. . . .

Neither recent nor distant history bears out Virginia's alleged pursuit of diversity through single-sex educational options. In 1839, when the State established VMI, a range of educational opportunities for men and women was scarcely contemplated. Higher education at the time was considered dangerous for women; reflecting widely held views about women's proper place, the Nation's first universities and colleges—for example, Harvard in Massachusetts, William and Mary in Virginia—admitted only men. . . .

Virginia describes the current absence of public single-sex higher education for women as "an historical anomaly." But the historical record indicates action more deliberate than anomalous: First, protection of women against higher education; next, schools for women far from equal in resources and stature to schools for men; finally, conversion of the separate schools to coeducation. The state legislature, prior to the advent of this controversy, had repealed "all Virginia statutes requiring individual institutions to admit only men or women." And in 1990, an official commission, "legislatively established to chart the future goals of higher education in Virginia," reaffirmed the policy "of affording broad access" while maintaining "autonomy and diversity." Significantly, the Commission reported:

> "Because colleges and universities provide opportunities for students to develop values and learn from role models, it is extremely important that they deal with faculty, staff, and students without regard to sex, race, or ethnic origin."

This statement, the Court of Appeals observed, "is the only explicit one that we have found in the record in which the Commonwealth has expressed itself with respect to gender distinctions."

Our 1982 decision in *Mississippi Univ. for Women* prompted VMI to reexamine its male-only admission policy. Virginia relies on that reexamination as a legitimate basis for maintaining VMI's single-sex character. A Mission Study Committee, appointed by the VMI Board of Visitors, studied the problem from October 1983 until May 1986, and in that month counseled against "change of VMI status as a single-sex college." Whatever internal purpose the Mission Study Committee served—and however well-meaning the framers of the report—we can hardly extract from that effort any state policy evenhandedly to advance diverse educational options. As the District Court observed, the Committee's analysis "primarily focused on anticipated difficulties in attracting females to VMI," and the report, overall, supplied "very little indication of how the conclusion was reached."

In sum, we find no persuasive evidence in this record that VMI's male-only admission policy "is in furtherance of a state policy of 'diversity.'" No such policy, the Fourth Circuit observed, can be discerned from the movement of all other public colleges and universities in Virginia away from single-sex education. That court also questioned "how one institution with autonomy, but with no authority over any other state institution, can give effect to a state policy of diversity among institutions." A purpose genuinely to advance an array of educational options, as the Court of Appeals recognized, is not served by VMI's historic and constant plan—a plan to "afford a unique educational benefit only to males." However "liberally" this plan serves the State's sons, it makes no provision whatever for her daughters. That is not equal protection.

B

Virginia next argues that VMI's adversative method of training provides educational benefits that cannot be made available, unmodified, to women. Alterations to accommodate women would necessarily be "radical," so "drastic," Virginia asserts, as to transform, indeed "destroy," VMI's program. Neither sex would be favored by the transformation, Virginia maintains: Men would be deprived of the unique opportunity currently available to them; women would not gain that opportunity because their participation would "eliminate the very aspects of [the] program that distinguish [VMI] from . . . other institutions of higher education in Virginia."

[It] is uncontested that women's admission would require accommodations, primarily in arranging housing assignments and physical training programs for female cadets. It is also undisputed, however, that "the VMI methodology could be used to educate women." ["Some] women," the expert testimony established, "are capable of all of the individual activities required of VMI cadets." The parties, furthermore, agree that "some women can meet the physical standards [VMI] now imposes on men." . . .

In support of its initial judgment for Virginia, a judgment rejecting all equal protection objections presented by the United States, the District Court made "findings" on "gender-based developmental differences." . . .

The United States does not challenge any expert witness estimation on average capacities or preferences of men and women. Instead, the United States emphasizes that time and again since this Court's turning point decision in Reed v. Reed, we have cautioned reviewing courts to take a "hard look" at generalizations or "tendencies" of the kind pressed by Virginia, and relied upon by the District Court. State actors controlling gates to opportunity, we have instructed, may not exclude qualified individuals based on "fixed notions concerning the roles and abilities of males and females." [*Mississippi Univ. for Women*]

It may be assumed, for purposes of this decision, that most women would not choose VMI's adversative method. As Fourth Circuit Judge Motz observed, however, in her dissent from the Court of Appeals' denial of rehearing en banc, it is also probable that "many men would not want to be educated in such an environment." (On that point, even our dissenting colleague might agree.) Education, to be sure, is not a "one size fits all" business. The issue, however, is not whether "women—or men—should be forced to attend VMI"; rather, the question is whether the State can constitutionally deny to women who have the will and capacity, the training and attendant opportunities that VMI uniquely affords.

The notion that admission of women would downgrade VMI's stature, destroy the adversative system and, with it, even the school, is a judgment hardly proved, a prediction hardly different from other "self-fulfilling prophecies," once routinely used to deny rights or opportunities. When women first sought admission to the bar and access to legal education, concerns of the same order were expressed. For example, in 1876, the Court of Common Pleas of Hennepin County, Minnesota, explained why women were thought ineligible for the practice of law. Women train and educate the young, the court said, which "forbids that they shall bestow that time (early and late) and labor, so essential in attaining to the eminence to which the true lawyer should ever aspire. It cannot therefore be said that the opposition of courts to the admission of females to practice . . . is to any extent the outgrowth of . . . 'old fogyism[.]' . . . It arises rather from a comprehension of the magnitude of the responsibilities connected with the successful practice of law, and a desire to grade up the profession." A like fear, according to a 1925 report, accounted for Columbia Law School's resistance to women's admission, although

> the faculty . . . never maintained that women could not master legal learning. . . . No, its argument has been . . . more practical. If women were admitted to the Columbia Law School, [the faculty] said, then the choicer, more manly and red-blooded graduates of our great universities would go to the Harvard Law School!" The Nation, Feb. 18, 1925, p.173. . . .

Women's successful entry into the federal military academies, and their participation in the Nation's military forces, indicate that Virginia's fears for the future of VMI may not be solidly grounded. The State's justification for excluding all women from "citizen-soldier" training for which some are qualified, in any event, cannot rank as "exceedingly persuasive," as we have explained and applied that standard.

Virginia and VMI trained their argument on "means" rather than "end," and thus misperceived our precedent. Single-sex education at VMI serves an "important governmental objective," they maintained, and exclusion of women is not only "substantially related," it is essential to that objective. By this notably circular argument, the "straightforward" test *Mississippi Univ. for Women* described was bent and bowed.

The State's misunderstanding and, in turn, the District Court's, is apparent from VMI's mission: to produce "citizen-soldiers," individuals "'imbued with love of learning, confident in the functions and attitudes of leadership, possessing a high sense of public service, advocates of the American democracy and free enterprise system, and ready . . . to defend their country in time of national peril.'"

Surely that goal is great enough to accommodate women, who today count as citizens in our American democracy equal in stature to men. Just as surely, the State's great goal is not substantially advanced by women's categorical exclusion, in total disregard of their individual merit, from the State's premier "citizen-soldier" corps.[16] Virginia, in sum, "has fallen far short of establishing the 'exceedingly persuasive justification,'" that must be the solid base for any gender-defined classification.

VI . . .

A . . .

Virginia chose not to eliminate, but to leave untouched, VMI's exclusionary policy. For women only, however, Virginia proposed a separate program, different in kind from VMI and unequal in tangible and intangible facilities. Having violated the Constitution's equal protection requirement, Virginia was obliged to show that its remedial proposal "directly addressed and related to" the violation, i.e., the equal protection denied to women ready, willing, and able to benefit from educational opportunities of the kind VMI offers. . . .

VWIL affords women no opportunity to experience the rigorous military training for which VMI is famed. Instead, the VWIL program "deemphasizes" military education, and uses a "cooperative method" of education "which reinforces self-esteem." . . .

Virginia maintains that these methodological differences are "justified pedagogically," based on "important differences between men and women in learning and developmental needs," "psychological and sociological differences" Virginia describes as "real" and "not stereotypes." . . .

16. VMI has successfully managed another notable change. The school admitted its first African-American cadets in 1968. See The VMI Story 347-349 (students no longer sing "Dixie," salute the Confederate flag or the tomb of General Robert E. Lee at ceremonies and sports events).

As earlier stated, generalizations about "the way women are," estimates of what is appropriate for most women, no longer justify denying opportunity to women whose talent and capacity place them outside the average description. Notably, Virginia never asserted that VMI's method of education suits most men. It is also revealing that Virginia accounted for its failure to make the VWIL experience "the entirely militaristic experience of VMI" on the ground that VWIL "is planned for women who do not necessarily expect to pursue military careers." By that reasoning, VMI's "entirely militaristic" program would be inappropriate for men in general or as a group, for "only about 15% of VMI cadets enter career military service."[19] . . .

B

In myriad respects other than military training, VWIL does not qualify as VMI's equal. VWIL's student body, faculty, course offerings, and facilities hardly match VMI's. Nor can the VWIL graduate anticipate the benefits associated with VMI's 157-year history, the school's prestige, and its influential alumni network. . . .

Virginia, in sum, while maintaining VMI for men only, has failed to provide any "comparable single-gender women's institution." Instead, the Commonwealth has created a VWIL program fairly appraised as a "pale shadow" of VMI in terms of the range of curricular choices and faculty stature, funding, prestige, alumni support and influence.

Virginia's VWIL solution is reminiscent of the remedy Texas proposed 50 years ago, in response to a state trial court's 1946 ruling that, given the equal protection guarantee, African Americans could not be denied a legal education at a state facility. See Sweatt v. Painter. Reluctant to admit African Americans to its flagship Univesity of Texas Law School, the State set up a separate school for Herman Sweatt and other black law students. . . .

More important than the tangible features, the [*Sweatt*] Court emphasized, are "those qualities which are incapable of objective measurement but which make for greatness" in a school, including "reputation of the faculty, experience of the administration, position and influence of the alumni, standing in the community, traditions and prestige." Facing the marked

19. Admitting women to VMI would undoubtedly require alterations necessary to afford members of each sex privacy from the other sex in living arrangements, and to adjust aspects of the physical training programs. Cf. note following 10 U.S.C. §4342 (academic and other standards for women admitted to the Military, Naval, and Air Force Academies "shall be the same as those required for male individuals, except for those minimum essential adjustments in such standards required because of physiological differences between male and female individuals"). Experience shows such adjustments are manageable. See U.S. Military Academy, A. Vitters, N. Kinzer, & J. Adams, Report of Admission of Women (Project Athena I-IV) (1977-1980) (4-year longitudinal study of the admission of women to West Point); Defense Advisory Committee on Women in the Services, Report on the Integration and Performance of Women at West Point 17-18 (1992). [Relocated footnote]

differences reported in the *Sweatt* opinion, the Court unanimously ruled that Texas had not shown "substantial equality in the [separate] educational opportunities" the State offered. Accordingly, the Court held, the Equal Protection Clause required Texas to admit African Americans to the University of Texas Law School. In line with *Sweatt*, we rule here that Virginia has not shown substantial equality in the separate educational opportunities the State supports at VWIL and VMI.

C . . .

Valuable as VWIL may prove for students who seek the program offered, Virginia's remedy affords no cure at all for the opportunities and advantages withheld from women who want a VMI education and can make the grade.[20] In sum, Virginia's remedy does not match the constitutional violation; the State has shown no "exceedingly persuasive justification" for withholding from women qualified for the experience premier training of the kind VMI affords.

VII . . .

A prime part of the history of our Constitution, historian Richard Morris recounted, is the story of the extension of constitutional rights and protections to people once ignored or excluded. [R. Morris, The Forging of the Union, 1781-1789 (1989).] VMI's story continued as our comprehension of "We the People" expanded. There is no reason to believe that the admission of women capable of all the activities required of VMI cadets would de-

20. Virginia's prime concern, it appears, is that "placing men and women into the adversative relationship inherent in the VMI program . . . would destroy, at least for that period of the adversative training, any sense of decency that still permeates the relationship between the sexes." It is an ancient and familiar fear. Compare In re Lavinia Goodell, 39 Wis. 232, 246 (1875) (denying female applicant's motion for admission to the bar of its court, Wisconsin Supreme Court explained: "Discussions are habitually necessary in courts of justice, which are unfit for female ears. The habitual presence of women at these would tend to relax the public sense of decency and propriety."), with Levine, Closing Comments, 6 Law & Inequality 41, 41 (1988) (presentation at Eighth Circuit Judicial Conference, Colorado Springs, Colorado, July 17, 1987) (footnotes omitted): "Plato questioned whether women should be afforded equal opportunity to become guardians, those elite Rulers of Platonic society. Ironically, in that most undemocratic system of government, the Republic, women's native ability to serve as guardians was not seriously questioned. The concern was over the wrestling and exercise class in which all candidates for guardianship had to participate, for rigorous physical and mental training were prerequisites to attain the exalted status of guardian. And in accord with Greek custom, those exercise classes were conducted in the nude. Plato concluded that their virtue would clothe the women's nakedness and that Platonic society would not thereby be deprived of the talent of qualified citizens for reasons of mere gender."

[Virginia,] not bound to ancient Greek custom in its "rigorous physical and mental training" programs, could more readily make the accommodations necessary to draw on "the talent of [all] qualified citizens."

stroy the Institute rather than enhance its capacity to serve the "more perfect Union."

For the reasons stated, the initial judgment of the Court of Appeals is affirmed, the final judgment of the Court of Appeals is reversed, and the case is remanded for further proceedings consistent with this opinion.

It is so ordered.

Justice Thomas took no part in the consideration or decision of this case.

CHIEF JUSTICE REHNQUIST, concurring in judgment.

The Court holds first that Virginia violates the Equal Protection Clause by maintaining [VMI's] all-male admissions policy, and second that establishing the [VWIL] program does not remedy that violation. While I agree with these conclusions, I disagree with the Court's analysis and so I write separately.

I

Two decades ago in Craig v. Boren, we announced that "to withstand constitutional challenge, . . . classifications by gender must serve important governmental objectives and must be substantially related to achievement of those objectives." We have adhered to that standard of scrutiny ever since. While the majority adheres to this test today, it also says that the State must demonstrate an "'exceedingly persuasive justification'" to support a gender-based classification. It is unfortunate that the Court thereby introduces an element of uncertainty respecting the appropriate test.

While terms like "important governmental objective" and "substantially related" are hardly models of precision, they have more content and specificity than does the phrase "exceedingly persuasive justification." That phrase is best confined, as it was first used, as an observation on the difficulty of meeting the applicable test, not as a formulation of the test itself. See, e.g., [Massachusetts v. Feeney] ("These precedents dictate that any state law overtly or covertly designed to prefer males over females in public employment require an exceedingly persuasive justification"). . . .

Our cases dealing with gender discrimination also require that the proffered purpose for the challenged law be the actual purpose. It is on this ground that the Court rejects the first of two justifications Virginia offers for VMI's single-sex admissions policy, namely, the goal of diversity among its public educational institutions. While I ultimately agree that the State has not carried the day with this justification, I disagree with the Court's method of analyzing the issue. . . .

I agree with the Court that there is scant evidence in the record that this was the real reason that Virginia decided to maintain VMI as men only. But, unlike the majority, I would consider only evidence that postdates our decision in *Hogan*, and would draw no negative inferences from the State's actions before that time. I think that after *Hogan*, the State was entitled to reconsider its policy with respect to VMI, and to not have earlier justifications, or lack thereof, held against it.

Even if diversity in educational opportunity were the State's actual objective, the State's position would still be problematic. The difficulty with its position is that the diversity benefited only one sex; there was single-sex public education available for men at VMI, but no corresponding single-sex public education available for women. When *Hogan* placed Virginia on notice that VMI's admissions policy possibly was unconstitutional, VMI could have dealt with the problem by admitting women; but its governing body felt strongly that the admission of women would have seriously harmed the institution's educational approach. Was there something else the State could have done to avoid an equal protection violation? Since the State did nothing, we do not have to definitively answer that question.

I do not think, however, that the State's options were as limited as the majority may imply. [VMI] had been in operation for over a century and a half, and had an established, successful and devoted group of alumni. No legislative wand could instantly call into existence a similar institution for women; and it would be a tremendous loss to scrap VMI's history and tradition. In the words of Grover Cleveland's second inaugural address, the State faced a condition, not a theory. And it was a condition that had been brought about, not through defiance of decisions construing gender bias under the Equal Protection Clause, but, until the decision in *Hogan*, a condition which had not appeared to offend the Constitution. Had Virginia made a genuine effort to devote comparable public resources to a facility for women, and followed through on such a plan, it might well have avoided an equal protection violation. I do not believe the State was faced with the stark choice of either admitting women to VMI, on the one hand, or abandoning VMI and starting from scratch for both men and women, on the other.

But [neither] the governing board of VMI nor the State took any action after 1982. If diversity in the form of single-sex, as well as coeducational, institutions of higher learning were to be available to Virginians, that diversity had to be available to women as well as to men. . . .

Virginia offers a second justification for the single-sex admissions policy: maintenance of the adversative method. I agree with the Court that this justification does not serve an important governmental objective. A State does not have substantial interest in the adversative methodology unless it is pedagogically beneficial. While considerable evidence shows that a single-sex education is pedagogically beneficial for some students, and hence a State may have a valid interest in promoting that methodology, there is no similar evidence in the record that an adversative method is pedagogically beneficial or is any more likely to produce character traits than other methodologies.

II

An adequate remedy in my opinion might be a demonstration by Virginia that its interest in educating men in a single-sex environment is matched by its interest in educating women in a single-sex institution. To demonstrate such, the State does not need to create two institutions with the same number of faculty PhD's, similar SAT scores, or comparable athletic fields. Nor would it necessarily require that the women's institution offer the same curriculum as the men's; one could be strong in computer science, the other could be strong in liberal arts. It would be a sufficient remedy, I think, if the two institutions offered the same quality of education and were of the same overall calibre.

If a state decides to create single-sex programs, the state would, I expect, consider the public's interest and demand in designing curricula. And rightfully so. But the state should avoid assuming demand based on stereotypes; it must not assume a priori, without evidence, that there would be no interest in a women's school of civil engineering, or in a men's school of nursing.

In the end, the women's institution Virginia proposes, VWIL, fails as a remedy, because it is distinctly inferior to the existing men's institution and will continue to be for the foreseeable future. VWIL simply is not, in any sense, the institution that VMI is. In particular, VWIL is a program appended to a private college, not a self-standing institution; and VWIL is substantially underfunded as compared to VMI. I therefore ultimately agree with the Court that Virginia has not provided an adequate remedy.

JUSTICE SCALIA, dissenting.

Today the Court shuts down an institution that has served the people of the Commonwealth of Virginia with pride and distinction for over a century and a half. To achieve that desired result, it rejects (contrary to our established practice) the factual findings of two courts below, sweeps aside the precedents of this Court, and ignores the history of our people. As to facts: it explicitly rejects the finding that there exist "gender-based developmental differences" supporting Virginia's restriction of the "adversative" method to only a men's institution, and the finding that the all-male composition of the Virginia Military Institute (VMI) is essential to that institution's character. As to precedent: it drastically revises our established standards for reviewing sex-based classifications. And as to history: it counts for nothing the long tradition, enduring down to the present, of men's military colleges supported by both States and the Federal Government.

Much of the Court's opinion is devoted to deprecating the closed-mindedness of our forebears with regard to women's education, and even with regard to the treatment of women in areas that have nothing to do with education. Closed-minded they were—as every age is, including our own, with regard to matters it cannot guess, because it simply does not consider them debatable. The virtue of a democratic system with a First Amendment is that it readily enables the people, over time, to be persuaded that what they took for granted is not so, and to change their laws accordingly. That system is destroyed if the smug assurances of each age are removed from the democratic process and written into the Constitution. So to counterbalance the Court's criticism of our ancestors, let me say a word in their praise: they left us free to change. The same cannot be said of this most illiberal Court, which has embarked on a course of inscribing one after another of the current preferences of the society (and in some cases only the counter-majoritarian preferences of the society's law-trained elite) into our Basic Law. Today it enshrines the notion that no substantial educational value is to be served by an all-men's military academy—so that the decision by the people of Virginia to maintain such an institution denies equal protection to women who cannot attend that institution but can attend others. Since it is entirely clear that the Constitution of the United States—the old one—takes no sides in this educational debate, I dissent.

I

I shall devote most of my analysis to evaluating the Court's opinion on the basis of our current equal-protection jurisprudence, which regards this Court as free to evaluate everything under the sun by applying one of three tests: "rational basis" scrutiny, intermediate scrutiny, or strict scrutiny. These tests are no more scientific than their names suggest, and a further element of randomness is added by the fact that it is largely up to us which test will be applied in each case. . . .

I have no problem with a system of abstract tests such as rational-basis, intermediate, and strict scrutiny (though I think we can do better than applying strict scrutiny and intermediate scrutiny whenever we feel like it). Such formulas are essential to evaluating whether the new restrictions that a changing society constantly imposes upon private conduct comport with that "equal protection" our society has always accorded in the past. But in my view the function of this Court is to preserve our society's values regarding (among other things) equal protection, not to revise them; to prevent backsliding from the degree of restriction the Constitution imposed upon democratic government, not to prescribe, on our own authority, progressively higher degrees. For that reason it is my view that, whatever abstract tests we may choose to devise, they cannot supersede—and indeed ought to be crafted so as to reflect—those constant and unbroken national traditions that embody the people's understanding of ambiguous constitutional texts. More specifically, it is my view that "when a practice not expressly prohibited by the text of the Bill of Rights bears the endorsement of a long tradition of open, widespread, and unchallenged use that dates back to the beginning of the Republic, we have no proper basis for striking it down." Rutan v. Republican Party of Ill., (Scalia, J., dissenting). . . .

The all-male constitution of VMI comes squarely within such a governing tradition. Founded by the Commonwealth of Virginia in 1839 and continuously maintained by it since, VMI has always admitted only men. And in that regard it has not been unusual. For almost all of VMI's more than a century and a half of existence, its single-sex status reflected the uniform practice for government-supported military colleges. [In] other words, the tradition of having government-funded military schools for men is as well rooted in the traditions of this country as the tradition of sending only men into military combat. The people may decide to change the one tradition, like the other, through democratic processes; but the assertion that either tradition has been unconstitutional through the centuries is not law, but politics-smuggled-into-law.

And the same applies, more broadly, to single-sex education in general, which, as I shall discuss, is threatened by today's decision with the cut-off of all state and federal support. . . .

Today, however, change is forced upon Virginia, and reversion to single-sex education is prohibited nationwide, not by democratic processes but by order of this Court. Even while bemoaning the sorry, bygone days of "fixed notions" concerning women's education, and the Court favors current notions so fixedly that it is willing to write them into the Constitution of the United States by application of custom-built "tests." This is not the interpretation of a Constitution, but the creation of one.

II

To reject the Court's disposition today, however, it is not necessary to accept my view that the Court's made-up tests cannot displace longstanding national traditions as the primary determinant of what the Constitution means. It is only necessary to apply honestly the test the Court has been applying to sex-based classifications for the past two decades. It is well settled, as Justice O'Connor stated some time ago for a unanimous Court, that we evaluate a statutory classification based on sex under a standard that lies "between the extremes of rational basis review and strict scrutiny." Clark v. Jeter. We have denominated this standard "intermediate scrutiny" and under it have inquired whether the statutory classification is "substantially related to an important governmental objective."

Before I proceed to apply this standard to VMI, I must comment upon the manner in which the Court avoids doing so. Notwithstanding our above-described precedents and their "'firmly established principles,'" the United States urged us to hold in this case "that strict scrutiny is the correct constitutional standard for evaluating classifications that deny opportunities to individuals based on their sex." [The] Court, while making no reference to the Government's argument, effectively accepts it. . . .

Only the amorphous "exceedingly persuasive justification" phrase, and not the standard elaboration of intermediate scrutiny, can be made to yield [the] conclusion that VMI's single-sex composition is unconstitutional because there exist several women (or, one would have to conclude under the Court's reasoning, a single woman) willing and able to undertake VMI's program. Intermediate scrutiny has never required a least-restrictive-means analysis, but only a "substantial relation" between the classification and the state interests that it serves. . . .

III . . .

A

It is beyond question that Virginia has an important state interest in providing effective college education for its citizens. That single-sex instruction is an approach substantially related to that interest should be evident enough from the long and continuing history in this country of men's and women's colleges. But beyond that, as the Court of Appeals here stated: "That single-gender education at the college level is beneficial to both sexes is a fact established in this case."

The evidence establishing that fact was overwhelming—indeed, "virtually uncontradicted" in the words of the court that received the evidence. [Virginia] demonstrated at trial that "[a] substantial body of contemporary scholarship and research supports the proposition that, although males and females have significant areas of developmental overlap, they also have differing developmental needs that are deep-seated." While no one questioned that for many students a coeducational environment was nonetheless not inappropriate, that could not obscure the demonstrated benefits of single-sex colleges. . . .

But besides its single-sex constitution, VMI is different from other colleges in another way. It employs a "distinctive educational method," sometimes referred to as the "adversative, or doubting, model of education." [It] was uncontested that "if the state were to establish a women's VMI-type [i.e., adversative] program, the program would attract an insufficient number of participants to make the program work," and it was found by the District Court that if Virginia were to include women in VMI, the school "would eventually find it necessary to drop the adversative system altogether." Thus, Virginia's options were an adversative method that excludes women or no adversative method at all.

[As] a theoretical matter, Virginia's educational interest would have been best served [by] six different types of public colleges—an all-men's, an all-women's, and a coeducational college run in the "adversative method," and an all-men's, an all-women's, and a coeducational college run in the "traditional method." But as a practical matter, of course, Virginia's financial resources, like any State's, are not limitless, and the Commonwealth must select among the available options. Virginia thus has decided to fund, in addition to some 14 coeducational 4-year colleges, one college that is run as an all-male school on the adversative model: the Virginia Military Institute. . . .

B

The Court today has no adequate response to this clear demonstration of the conclusion produced by application of intermediate scrutiny. Rather, it relies on a series of contentions that are irrelevant or erroneous as a matter of law, foreclosed by the record in this case, or both. . . .

[The] Court suggests that Virginia's claimed purpose in maintaining VMI as an all-male institution—its asserted interest in promoting diversity of educational options—is not "genuine," but is a pretext for discriminating against women. To support this charge, the Court would have to impute that base motive to VMI's Mission Study Committee, which conducted a 3-year study from 1983 to 1986 and recommended to VMI's Board of Visitors that the school remain all-male. The Committee, a majority of whose members consisted of non-VMI graduates, "read materials on education and on women in the military," "made site visits to single-sex and newly coeducational institutions" including West Point and the Naval Academy, and "considered the reasons that other institutions had changed from single-sex to coeducational status"; its work was praised as "thorough" in the accreditation review of VMI conducted by the Southern Association of Colleges and Schools. [The] relevance of the Mission Study Committee is that its very creation, its sober 3-year study, and the analysis it produced, utterly refute the claim that VMI has elected to maintain its all-male student-body composition for some misogynistic reason. . . .

[In] addition to disparaging Virginia's claim that VMI's single-sex status serves a state interest in diversity, the Court finds fault with Virginia's failure to offer education based on the adversative training method to women. . . .

Ultimately, [the] Court does not deny the evidence supporting [the District Court's findings on gender-based developmental differences]. It instead makes evident that the parties to this case could have saved themselves a great deal of time, trouble, and expense by omitting a trial. The Court simply dispenses with the evidence submitted at trial—it never says that a single finding of the District Court is clearly erroneous—in favor of the Justices' own view of the [world].

It is not too much to say that this approach to the case has rendered the trial a sham. But treating the evidence as irrelevant is absolutely necessary for the Court to reach its conclusion. Not a single witness contested, for example, Virginia's "substantial body of 'exceedingly persuasive' evidence . . . that some students, both male and female, benefit from attending a single-sex college" and "[that] for those students, the opportunity to attend a single-sex college is a valuable one, likely to lead to better academic and professional achievement." Even the United States' expert witness "called himself a 'believer in single-sex education,' " although it was his "personal, philosophical preference," not one "born of educational-benefit considerations," "that single-sex education should be provided only by the private sector." . . .

[The] Court argues that VMI would not have to change very much if it were to admit women. The principal response to that argument is that it is irrelevant: If VMI's single-sex status is substantially related to the government's important educational objectives, as I have demonstrated above and as the Court refuses to discuss, that concludes the inquiry. There should be no debate in the federal judiciary over "how much" VMI would be required to change if it admitted women and whether that would constitute "too much" change.

But if such a debate were relevant, the Court would certainly be on the losing side. The District Court found as follows: "The evidence establishes that key elements of the adversative VMI educational system, with its focus on barracks life, would be fundamentally altered, and the distinctive ends of the system would be thwarted, if VMI were forced to admit females and to make changes necessary to accommodate their needs and interests." Changes that the District Court's detailed analysis found would be required include new allowances for personal privacy in the barracks, such as locked doors and coverings on windows, which would detract from VMI's approach of regulating minute details of student behavior, "contradict the principle that everyone is constantly subject to scrutiny by everyone else," and impair VMI's "total egalitarian approach" under which every student must be "treated alike"; changes in the physical training program, which would reduce "the intensity and aggressiveness of the current program"; and various modifications in other respects of the adversative training program which permeates student life. . . .

[Finally,] the absence of a precise "all-women's analogue" to VMI is irrelevant. In Mississippi Univ. for Women v. Hogan, we attached no constitutional significance to the absence of an all-male nursing school. . . .

Although there is no precise female-only analogue to VMI, Virginia has created during this litigation the Virginia Women's Institute for Leadership (VWIL), a state-funded all-women's program run by Mary Baldwin College. I have thus far said nothing about VWIL because it is, under our established test, irrelevant, so long as VMI's all-male character is "substantially related" to an important state goal. But VWIL now exists, and the Court's treatment of it shows how far-reaching today's decision is.

VWIL was carefully designed by professional educators who have long experience in educating young women. The program rejects the proposition that there is a "difference in the respective spheres and destinies of man and woman," Bradwell v. State, and is designed to "provide an all-female program that will achieve substantially similar outcomes [to VMI's] in an all-female environment," After holding a trial where voluminous evidence was submitted and making detailed findings of fact, the District Court concluded that "there is a legitimate pedagogical basis for the different means employed [by VMI and VWIL] to achieve the substantially similar ends." . . .

IV

As is frequently true, the Court's decision today will have consequences that extend far beyond the parties to the case. What I take to be the Court's unease with these consequences, and its resulting unwillingness to acknowledge them, cannot alter the reality.

A

Under the constitutional principles announced and applied today, single-sex public education is unconstitutional. . . .

[The] rationale of today's decision is sweeping: for sex-based classifications, a redefinition of intermediate scrutiny that makes it indistinguishable from strict scrutiny. Indeed, the Court indicates that if any program restricted to one sex is "unique," it must be opened to members of the opposite sex "who have the will and capacity" to participate in it. I suggest that the single-sex program that will not be capable of being characterized as "unique" is not only unique but nonexistent.[8]

8. In this regard, I note that the Court—which I concede is under no obligation to do so—provides no example of a program that would pass muster under its reasoning today: not even, for example, a football or wrestling program. On the Court's theory, any woman ready, willing, and physically able to participate in such a program would, as a constitutional matter, be entitled to do so.

In any event, regardless of whether the Court's rationale leaves some small amount of room for lawyers to argue, it ensures that single-sex public education is functionally dead. The costs of litigating the constitutionality of a single-sex education program, and the risks of ultimately losing that litigation, are simply too high to be embraced by public officials. [The] enemies of single-sex education have won; by persuading only seven Justices (five would have been enough) that their view of the world is enshrined in the Constitution, they have effectively imposed that view on all 50 States.

This is especially regrettable because, as the District Court here determined, educational experts in recent years have increasingly come to "support [the] view that substantial educational benefits flow from a single-gender environment, be it male or female, that cannot be replicated in a coeducational setting." "The evidence in this case," for example, "is virtually uncontradicted" to that effect. Until quite recently, some public officials have attempted to institute new single-sex programs, at least as experiments. In 1991, for example, the Detroit Board of Education announced a program to establish three boys-only schools for inner-city youth; it was met with a lawsuit, a preliminary injunction was swiftly entered by a District Court that purported to rely on Hogan, and the Detroit Board of Education voted to abandon the litigation and thus abandon the plan. Today's opinion assures that no such experiment will be tried again.

B

There are few extant single-sex public educational programs. The potential of today's decision for widespread disruption of existing institutions lies in its application to private single-sex education. Government support is immensely important to private educational institutions. [Charitable] status under the tax laws is also highly significant for private educational institutions, and it is certainly not beyond the Court that rendered today's decision to hold that a donation to a single-sex college should be deemed contrary to public policy and therefore not deductible if the college discriminates on the basis of sex. . . .

The only hope for state-assisted single-sex private schools is that the Court will not apply in the future the principles of law it has applied today. That is a substantial hope, I am happy and ashamed to say. After all, did not the Court today abandon the principles of law it has applied in our earlier sex-classification cases? And does not the Court positively invite private colleges to rely upon our ad-hocery by assuring them this case is "unique"? I would not advise the foundation of any new single-sex college (especially an all-male one) with the expectation of being allowed to receive any government support; but it is too soon to abandon in despair those single-sex colleges already in existence. It will certainly be possible for this Court to write a future opinion that ignores the broad principles of law set forth today, and that characterizes as utterly dispositive the opinion's perceptions that VMI was a uniquely prestigious all-male institution, conceived in chauvinism, etc., etc. I will not join that opinion.

Justice Brandeis said it is "one of the happy incidents of the federal system that a single courageous State may, if its citizens choose, serve as a laboratory; and try novel social and economic experiments without risk to the rest of the country." New State Ice Co. v. Liebmann (dissenting opinion). But it is one of the unhappy incidents of the federal system that a self-righteous Supreme Court, acting on its Members' personal view of what would make a "more perfect Union," (a criterion only slightly more restrictive than a "more perfect world"), can impose its own favored social and economic dispositions nationwide. As today's disposition, and others this single Term, show, this places it beyond the power of a "single courageous State," not only to introduce novel dispositions that the Court frowns upon, but to reintroduce, or indeed even adhere to, disfavored dispositions that are centuries old. See, Romer v. Evans, 517 U. S. — [116 S. Ct. 1620] (1996). The sphere of self-government reserved to the people of the Republic is progressively narrowed.

In the course of this dissent, I have referred approvingly to the opinion of my former colleague, Justice Powell, in Mississippi Univ. for Women v. Hogan. Many of the points made in his dissent apply with equal force here—in particular, the criticism of judicial opinions that purport to be "narrow" but whose "logic" is "sweeping." But there is one statement with which I cannot agree. Justice Powell observed that the Court's decision in *Hogan*, which struck down a single-sex program offered by the Mississippi University for Women, had thereby "left without honor . . . an element of diversity that has characterized much of American education and enriched much of American life." Today's decision does not leave VMI without honor; no court opinion can do that.

In an odd sort of way, it is precisely VMI's attachment to such old-fashioned concepts as manly "honor" that has made it, and the system it represents, the target of those who today succeed in abolishing public single-sex education. The record contains a booklet that all first-year VMI students (the so-called "rats") were required to keep in their possession at all times. Near the end there appears the following period-piece, entitled "The Code of a Gentleman":

> Without a strict observance of the fundamental Code of Honor, no man, no matter how "polished," can be considered a gentleman. The honor of a gentleman demands the inviolability of his word, and the incorruptibility of his prin-

> ciples. He is the descendant of the knight, the crusader; he is the defender of the defenseless and the champion of justice . . . or he is not a Gentleman.
>
> A Gentleman . . .
>
> Does not discuss his family affairs in public or with acquaintances.
>
> Does not speak more than casually about his girl friend.
>
> Does not go to a lady's house if he is affected by alcohol. He is temperate in the use of alcohol.
>
> Does not lose his temper; nor exhibit anger, fear, hate, embarrassment, ardor or hilarity in public.
>
> Does not hail a lady from a club window.
>
> A gentleman never discusses the merits or demerits of a lady.
>
> Does not mention names exactly as he avoids the mention of what things cost.
>
> Does not borrow money from a friend, except in dire need. Money borrowed is a debt of honor, and must be repaid as promptly as possible. Debts incurred by a deceased parent, brother, sister or grown child are assumed by honorable men as a debt of honor.
>
> Does not display his wealth, money or possessions.
>
> Does not put his manners on and off, whether in the club or in a ballroom. He treats people with courtesy, no matter what their social position may be.
>
> Does not slap strangers on the back nor so much as lay a finger on a lady.
>
> Does not "lick the boots of those above" nor "kick the face of those below him on the social ladder."
>
> Does not take advantage of another's helplessness or ignorance and assumes that no gentleman will take advantage of him.
>
> A Gentleman respects the reserves of others, but demands that others respect those which are his.
>
> A Gentleman can become what he wills to be. . . .

I do not know whether the men of VMI lived by this Code; perhaps not. But it is powerfully impressive that a public institution of higher education still in existence sought to have them do so. I do not think any of us, women included, will be better off for its destruction.

E. EQUAL PROTECTION METHODOLOGY: OTHER CANDIDATES FOR HEIGHTENED SCRUTINY

Page 780. Before Section 4, add the following:

In the case that follows, the Court, for the first time in its history, invalidated a measure on the ground that it discriminated against homosexuals. Consider the extent to which the Court's decision requires rethinking of lower court decisions about homosexual marriage, criminalization of homosexual sodomy, and service by homosexuals in the military.

ROMER v. EVANS

116 S. Ct. 1620 (1996)

JUSTICE KENNEDY delivered the opinion of the Court.

One century ago, the first Justice Harlan admonished this Court that the Constitution "neither knows nor tolerates classes among citizens." Plessy v. Ferguson (dissenting opinion). Unheeded then, those words now are understood to state a commitment to the law's neutrality where the rights of persons are at stake. The Equal Protection Clause enforces this principle and today requires us to hold invalid a provision of Colorado's Constitution.

I

["Amendment 2" was added to the state constitution by a statewide referendum held in 1992. It was enacted after a number of Colorado municipalities had adopted ordinances prohibiting discrimination on the basis of sexual orientation in many transactions and activities such as housing, employment, education, public accommodations, and health and welfare services. It provided:

No Protected Status Based on Homosexual, Lesbian, or Bisexual Orientation

> Neither the State of Colorado, through any of its branches or departments, nor any of its agencies, political subdivisions, municipalities or school districts, shall enact, adopt or enforce any statute, regulation, ordinance or policy whereby homosexual, lesbian or bisexual orientation, conduct, practices or relationships shall constitute or otherwise be the basis of or entitle any person or class of persons to have or claim any minority status, quota preferences, protected status or claim of discrimination. This Section of the Constitution shall be in all respects self-executing.

[The Colorado Supreme Court held that Amendment 2 was subject to strict scrutiny under the equal protection clause on the ground that it impinged on the right of homosexuals to participate in the political process.] On remand, the State advanced various arguments in an effort to show that Amendment 2 was narrowly tailored to serve compelling interests, but the trial court found none sufficient. It enjoined enforcement of Amendment 2, and the Supreme Court of Colorado, in a second opinion, affirmed the ruling. We granted certiorari and now affirm the judgment, but on a rationale different from that adopted by the State Supreme Court.

II

The State's principal argument in defense of Amendment 2 is that it puts gays and lesbians in the same position as all other persons. So, the State says, the measure does no more than deny homosexuals special rights. This reading of the amendment's language is implausible. We rely not upon our own interpretation of the amendment but upon the authoritative construction of Colorado's Supreme Court. The state court, deeming it unnecessary to determine the full extent of the amendment's reach, found it invalid even on a modest reading of its implications. The critical discussion of the amendment [is] as follows:

> The immediate objective of Amendment 2 is, at a minimum, to repeal existing statutes, regulations, ordinances, and policies of state and local entities that barred discrimination based on sexual orientation.
>
> The "ultimate effect" of Amendment 2 is to prohibit any governmental entity from adopting similar, or more protective statutes, regulations, ordinances, or policies in the future unless the state constitution is first amended to permit such measures.

Sweeping and comprehensive is the change in legal status effected by this law. So much is evident from the ordinances that the Colorado Supreme Court declared would be void by operation of Amendment 2. Homosexuals, by state decree, are put in a solitary class with respect to transactions and relations in both the private and governmental spheres. The amendment withdraws from homosexuals, but no others, specific legal protection from the injuries caused by discrimination, and it forbids reinstatement of these laws and policies.

The change that Amendment 2 works in the legal status of gays and lesbians in the private sphere is far-reaching, both on its own terms and when considered in light of the structure and operation of modern anti-discrimination laws. That structure is well illustrated by contemporary statutes and ordinances prohibiting discrimination by providers of public accommodations. "At common law, innkeepers, smiths, and others who 'made profession of a public employment,' were prohibited from refusing, without good reason, to serve a customer." Hurley v. Irish-American Gay, Lesbian and Bisexual Group of Boston, Inc., 515 U.S. —, — [115 S. Ct. 2338] (1995). The duty was a general one and did not specify protection for particular groups. The common law rules, however, proved insufficient in many instances, and it was settled early that the Fourteenth Amendment did not give Congress a general power to prohibit discrimination in public accommodations. In consequence, most States have chosen to counter discrimination by enacting detailed statutory schemes.

Colorado's state and municipal laws typify this emerging tradition of statutory protection and follow a consistent pattern. The laws first enumerate the persons or entities subject to a duty not to discriminate. The list goes well beyond the entities covered by the common law. The Boulder ordinance, for example, has a comprehensive definition of entities deemed places of "public accommodation." They include "any place of business engaged in any sales to the general public and any place that offers services, facilities, privileges, or advantages to the general public or that receives financial support through solicitation of the general public or through governmental subsidy of any kind." . . .

These statutes and ordinances also depart from the common law by enumerating the groups or persons within their ambit of protection. Enumeration is the essential device used to make the duty not to discriminate concrete and to provide guidance for those who must comply. In following this approach, Colorado's state and local governments have not limited anti-discrimination laws to groups that have so far been given the protection of heightened equal protection scrutiny under our cases. Rather, they set forth an extensive catalogue of traits which cannot be the basis for discrimination, including age, military status, marital status, pregnancy, parenthood, custody of a minor child, political affiliation, physical or mental disability of an individual or of his or her associates and, in recent times, sexual orientation.

Amendment 2 bars homosexuals from securing protection against the injuries that these public-accommodations laws address. That in itself is a severe consequence, but there is more. Amendment 2, in addition, nullifies specific legal protections for this targeted class in all transactions in housing, sale of real estate, insurance, health and welfare services, private education, and employment.

Not confined to the private sphere, Amendment 2 also operates to repeal and forbid all laws or policies providing specific protection for gays or lesbians from discrimination by every level of Colorado government. The State Supreme Court cited two examples of protections in the governmental sphere that are now rescinded and may not be reintroduced. The first is Colorado Executive Order D0035 (1990), which forbids employment discrimination against "'all state employees, classified and exempt' on the basis of sexual orientation." Also repealed, and now forbidden, are "various provisions prohibiting discrimination based on sexual orientation at state colleges." The repeal of these measures and the prohibition against their future reenactment demonstrates that Amendment 2 has the same force and effect in Colorado's governmental sector as it does elsewhere and that it applies to policies as well as ordinary legislation.

Amendment 2's reach may not be limited to specific laws passed for the benefit of gays and lesbians. It is a fair, if not necessary, inference from the broad language of the amendment that it deprives gays and lesbians even of the protection of general laws and policies that prohibit arbitrary discrimination in governmental and private settings. At some point in the systematic administration of these laws, an official must determine whether homosexuality is an arbitrary and thus forbidden basis for decision. Yet a decision to that effect would itself amount to a policy prohibiting discrimination on the basis of homosexuality, and so would appear to be no more valid under Amendment 2 than the specific prohibitions against discrimination the state court held invalid.

If this consequence follows from Amendment 2, as its broad language suggests, it would compound the constitutional difficulties the law creates. The state court did not decide whether the amendment has this effect, however, and neither need we. In the course of rejecting the argument that Amendment 2 is intended to conserve resources to fight discrimination against suspect classes, the Colorado Supreme Court made the limited observation that the amendment is not intended to affect many anti-discrimination laws protecting non-suspect classes, In our view that does not resolve the issue. In any event, even if, as we doubt, homosexuals could find some safe harbor in laws of general application, we cannot accept the view that Amendment 2's prohibition on specific legal protections does no more than deprive homosexuals of special rights. To the contrary, the amendment imposes a special disability upon those persons alone. Homosexuals are forbidden the safeguards that others enjoy or may seek without constraint. They can obtain specific protection against discrimination only by enlisting the citizenry of Colorado to amend the state constitution or perhaps, on the State's view, by trying to pass helpful laws of general applicability. This is so no matter how local or discrete the harm, no matter how public and widespread the injury. We find nothing special in the protections Amendment 2 withholds. These are protections taken for granted by most people either because they already have them or do not need them; these are protections against exclusion from an almost limitless number of transactions and endeavors that constitute ordinary civic life in a free society.

III

The Fourteenth Amendment's promise that no person shall be denied the equal protection of the laws must co-exist with the practical necessity that most legislation classifies for one purpose or another, with resulting disadvantage to various groups or persons. We have attempted to reconcile the principle with the reality by stating that, if a law neither burdens a fundamental right nor targets a suspect class, we will uphold the legislative classification so long as it bears a rational relation to some legitimate end.

Amendment 2 fails, indeed defies, even this conventional inquiry. First, the amendment has the peculiar property of imposing a broad and undifferentiated disability on a single named group, an exceptional and, as we shall explain, invalid form of legislation. Second, its sheer breadth is so discontinuous with the reasons offered for it that the amendment seems inexplicable by anything but animus toward the class that it affects; it lacks a rational relationship to legitimate state interests.

Taking the first point, even in the ordinary equal protection case calling for the most deferential of standards, we insist on knowing the relation between the classification adopted and the object to be attained. The search for the link between classification and objective gives substance to the Equal Protection Clause; it provides guidance and discipline for the legislature, which is entitled to know what sorts of laws it can pass; and it marks the limits of our own authority. In the ordinary case, a law will be sustained if it can be said to advance a legitimate government interest, even if the law seems unwise or works to the disadvantage of a particular group, or if the rationale for it seems tenuous. See New Orleans v. Dukes (tourism benefits justified classification favoring pushcart vendors of certain longevity); Williamson v. Lee Optical of Okla., Inc., (assumed health concerns justified law favoring optometrists over opticians); Railway Express Agency, Inc. v. New York (potential traffic hazards justified exemption of vehicles advertising the owner's products from general advertising ban); Kotch v. Board of River Port Pilot Comm'rs for Port of New Orleans, (licensing scheme that disfavored persons unrelated to current river boat pilots justified by possible efficiency and safety benefits of a closely knit pilotage system). The laws challenged in the cases just cited were narrow enough in scope and grounded in a sufficient factual context for us to ascertain that there existed some relation between the classification and the purpose it served. By requiring that the classification bear a rational relationship to an independent and legitimate legislative end, we ensure that classifications are not drawn for the purpose of disadvantaging the group burdened by the law.

Amendment 2 confounds this normal process of judicial review. It is at once too narrow and too broad. It identifies persons by a single trait and then denies them protection across the board. The resulting disqualification of a class of persons from the right to seek specific protection from the law is unprecedented in our jurisprudence. The absence of precedent for Amendment 2 is itself instructive; "discriminations of an unusual character especially suggest careful consideration to determine whether they are obnoxious to the constitutional provision." Louisville Gas & Elec. Co. v. Coleman, 277 U.S. 32, 37-38, (1928).

It is not within our constitutional tradition to enact laws of this sort. Central both to the idea of the rule of law and to our own Constitution's guarantee of equal protection is the principle that government and each of its parts remain open on impartial terms to all who seek its assistance. "'Equal protection of the laws is not achieved through indiscriminate imposition of inequalities.'" Sweatt v. Painter, (quoting Shelley v. Kraemer). Respect for this principle explains why laws singling out a certain class of citizens for disfavored legal status or general hardships are rare. A law declaring that in general it shall be more difficult for one group of citizens than for all others to seek aid from the government is itself a denial of equal protection of the laws in the most literal sense. "The guaranty of 'equal protection of the laws is a pledge of the protection of equal laws.'" Skinner v. Oklahoma ex rel. Williamson, (quoting Yick Wo v. Hopkins).

Davis v. Beason, 133 U.S. 333, (1890), not cited by the parties but relied upon by the dissent, is not evidence that Amendment 2 is within our constitutional tradition, and any reliance upon it as authority for sustaining the amendment is misplaced. In Davis, the Court approved an Idaho territorial statute denying Mormons, polygamists, and advocates of polygamy the right to vote and to hold office because, as the Court construed the statute, it "simply excludes from the privilege of voting, or of holding any office of honor, trust or profit, those who have been convicted of certain offences, and those who advocate a practical resistance to the laws of the Territory and justify and approve the commission of crimes forbidden by it." To the extent Davis held that persons advocating a certain practice may be denied the right to vote, it is no longer good law. Brandenburg v. Ohio, 395 U.S. 444, (1969) (per curiam). To the extent it held that the groups designated in the statute may be deprived of the right to vote because of their status, its ruling could not stand without surviving strict scrutiny, a most doubtful outcome. Dunn v. Blumstein, 405 U.S. 330, 337, (1972). To the extent *Davis* held that a convicted felon may be denied the right to vote, its holding is not implicated by our decision and is unexceptionable. See Richardson v. Ramirez, 418 U.S. 24 (1974).

A second and related point is that laws of the kind now before us raise the inevitable inference that the disadvantage imposed is born of animosity toward the class of persons affected. "If the constitutional conception of 'equal protection of the laws' means anything, it must at the very least mean that a bare . . . desire to harm a politically unpopular group cannot constitute a legitimate governmental interest." Department of Agriculture v. Moreno. Even laws enacted for broad and ambitious purposes often can be explained by reference to legitimate public policies which justify the incidental disadvantages they impose on certain persons. Amendment 2, however, in making a general announcement that gays and lesbians shall not have any particular protections from the law, inflicts on them immediate, continuing, and real injuries that outrun and belie any legitimate justifications that may be claimed for it. We conclude that, in addition to the far-reaching deficiencies of Amendment 2 that we have noted, the principles it offends, in another sense, are conventional and venerable; a law must bear a rational relationship to a legitimate governmental purpose, and Amendment 2 does not.

The primary rationale the State offers for Amendment 2 is respect for other citizens' freedom of association, and in particular the liberties of landlords or employers who have personal or religious objections to homosexuality. Colorado also cites its interest in conserving resources to fight discrimination against other groups. The breadth of the Amendment is so far removed from these particular justifications that we find it impossible to credit them. We cannot say that Amendment 2 is directed to any identifiable legitimate purpose or discrete objective. It is a status-based enactment divorced from any factual context from which we could discern a relationship to legitimate state interests; it is a classification of persons undertaken for its own sake, something the Equal Protection Clause does not permit. "Class legislation . . . [is] obnoxious to the prohibitions of the Fourteenth Amendment. . . ." Civil Rights Cases, 109 U.S. at 24.

We must conclude that Amendment 2 classifies homosexuals not to further a proper legislative end but to make them unequal to everyone else. This Colorado cannot do. A State cannot so deem a class of persons a stranger to its laws. Amendment 2 violates the Equal Protection Clause, and the judgment of the Supreme Court of Colorado is affirmed.

JUSTICE SCALIA, with whom [CHIEF JUSTICE REHNQUIST] and JUSTICE THOMAS join, dissenting.

The Court has mistaken a Kulturkampf for a fit of spite. The constitutional amendment before us here is not the manifestation of a "'bare . . . desire to harm'" homosexuals, but is rather a modest attempt by seemingly tolerant Coloradans to preserve traditional sexual mores against the efforts of a politically powerful minority to revise those mores through use of the laws. That objective, and the means chosen to achieve it, are not only unimpeachable under any constitutional doctrine hitherto pronounced (hence the opinion's heavy reliance upon principles of righteousness rather than judicial holdings); they have been specifically approved by the Congress of the United States and by this Court.

In holding that homosexuality cannot be singled out for disfavorable treatment, the Court contradicts a decision, unchallenged here, pronounced only 10 years ago, see Bowers v. Hardwick, and places the prestige of this institution behind the proposition that opposition to homosexuality is as reprehensible as racial or religious bias. Whether it is or not is precisely the cultural debate that gave rise to the Colorado constitutional amendment (and to the preferential laws against which the amendment was directed). Since the Constitution of the United States says nothing about this subject, it is left to be resolved by normal democratic means, including the democratic adoption of provisions in state constitutions. This Court has no business imposing upon all Americans the resolution favored by the elite class from which the Members of this institution are selected, pronouncing that "animosity" toward homosexuality, is evil. I vigorously dissent.

I

Let me first discuss Part II of the Court's opinion, its longest section, which is devoted to rejecting the State's arguments that Amendment 2 "puts gays and lesbians in the same position as all other persons," and "does no more than deny homosexuals special rights." The Court concludes that this reading of Amendment 2's language is "implausible" under the "authoritative construction" given Amendment 2 by the Supreme Court of Colorado.

In reaching this conclusion, the Court considers it unnecessary to decide the validity of the State's argument that Amendment 2 does not deprive homosexuals of the "protection [afforded by] general laws and policies that prohibit arbitrary discrimination in governmental and private settings." I agree that we need not resolve that dispute, because the Supreme Court of Colorado has resolved it for us. [The] Colorado court stated:

> It is significant to note that Colorado law currently proscribes discrimination against persons who are not suspect classes, including discrimination based on age, marital or family status, veterans' status, and for any legal, off-duty conduct such as smoking tobacco. Of course Amendment 2 is not intended to have any effect on this legislation, but seeks only to prevent the adoption of anti-discrimination laws intended to protect gays, lesbians, and bisexuals.

The Court utterly fails to distinguish this portion of the Colorado court's opinion. [The] clear import of the Colorado court's conclusion [is] that "general laws and policies that prohibit arbitrary discrimination" would continue to prohibit discrimination on the basis of homosexual conduct as well. This analysis, which is fully in accord with (indeed, follows inescapably from) the text of the constitutional provision, lays to rest such horribles, raised in the course of oral argument, as the prospect that assaults upon homosexuals could not be prosecuted. The amendment prohibits special treatment of homosexuals, and nothing more. It would not affect, for example, a requirement of state law that pensions be paid to all retiring state employees with a certain length of service; homosexual employees, as well as others, would be entitled to that benefit. But it would prevent the State or any municipality from making death-benefit payments to the "life partner" of a homosexual when it does not make such payments to the long-time roommate of a nonhomosexual employee. Or again, it does not affect the requirement of the State's general insurance laws that customers be afforded coverage without discrimination unrelated to anticipated risk. Thus, homosexuals could not be denied coverage, or charged a greater premium, with respect to auto collision insurance; but neither the State nor any municipality could require that distinctive health insurance risks associated with homosexuality (if there are any) be ignored.

Despite all of its hand-wringing about the potential effect of Amendment 2 on general antidiscrimination laws, the Court's opinion ultimately does not dispute all this, but assumes it to be true. The only denial of equal treatment it contends homosexuals have suffered is this: They may not obtain preferential treatment without amending the state constitution. That is to say, the principle underlying the Court's opinion is that one who is accorded equal treatment under the laws, but cannot as readily as others obtain preferential treatment under the laws, has been denied equal protection of the laws. If merely stating this alleged "equal protection" violation does not suffice to refute it, our constitutional jurisprudence has achieved terminal silliness.

The central thesis of the Court's reasoning is that any group is denied equal protection when, to obtain advantage (or, presumably, to avoid disadvantage), it must have recourse to a more general and hence more difficult level of political decisionmaking than others. The world has never heard of such a principle, which is why the Court's opinion is so long on emotive utterance and so short on relevant legal citation. And it seems to me most unlikely that any multilevel democracy can function under such a principle. For whenever a disadvantage is imposed, or conferral of a benefit is prohibited, at one of the higher levels of democratic decisionmaking (i.e., by the state legislature rather than local government, or by the people at large in the state constitution rather than the legislature), the affected group has (under this theory) been denied equal protection. To take the simplest of examples, consider a state law prohibiting the award of municipal contracts to relatives of mayors or city councilmen. Once such a law is passed, the group composed of such relatives must, in order to get the benefit of city contracts, persuade the state legislature—unlike all other citizens, who need only persuade the municipality. It is ridiculous to consider this a denial of equal protection, which is why the Court's theory is unheard-of.

The Court might reply that the example I have given is not a denial of equal protection only because the same "rational basis" (avoidance of corruption) which renders constitutional the substantive discrimination against relatives (i.e., the fact that they alone cannot obtain city contracts) also automatically suffices to sustain what might be called the electoral-procedural discrimination against them (i.e., the fact that they must go to the state level to get this changed). This is of course a perfectly reasonable response, and would explain why "electoral-procedural discrimination" has not hitherto been heard of: a law that is valid in its substance is automatically valid in its level of enactment. But the Court cannot afford to make this argument, for as I shall discuss next, there is no doubt of a rational basis for the substance of the prohibition at issue here. The Court's entire novel theory rests upon the proposition that there is something special—

something that cannot be justified by normal "rational basis" analysis—in making a disadvantaged group (or a nonpreferred group) resort to a higher decisionmaking level. That proposition finds no support in law or logic.

II

I turn next to whether there was a legitimate rational basis for the substance of the constitutional amendment—for the prohibition of special protection for homosexuals. It is unsurprising that the Court avoids discussion of this question, since the answer is so obviously yes. The case most relevant to the issue before us today is not even mentioned in the Court's opinion: In Bowers v. Hardwick, we held that the Constitution does not prohibit what virtually all States had done from the founding of the Republic until very recent years—making homosexual conduct a crime. That holding is unassailable, except by those who think that the Constitution changes to suit current fashions. But in any event it is a given in the present case: Respondents' briefs did not urge overruling Bowers, and at oral argument respondents' counsel expressly disavowed any intent to seek such overruling. If it is constitutionally permissible for a State to make homosexual conduct criminal, surely it is constitutionally permissible for a State to enact other laws merely disfavoring homosexual conduct. [And] a fortiori it is constitutionally permissible for a State to adopt a provision not even disfavoring homosexual conduct, but merely prohibiting all levels of state government from bestowing special protections upon homosexual conduct. Respondents (who, unlike the Court, cannot afford the luxury of ignoring inconvenient precedent) counter *Bowers* with the argument that a greater-includes-the-lesser rationale cannot justify Amendment 2's application to individuals who do not engage in homosexual acts, but are merely of homosexual "orientation." . . .

But assuming that, in Amendment 2, a person of homosexual "orientation" is someone who does not engage in homosexual conduct but merely has a tendency or desire to do so, *Bowers* still suffices to establish a rational basis for the provision. If it is rational to criminalize the conduct, surely it is rational to deny special favor and protection to those with a self-avowed tendency or desire to engage in the conduct. Indeed, where criminal sanctions are not involved, homosexual "orientation" is an acceptable stand-in for homosexual conduct. A State "does not violate the Equal Protection Clause merely because the classifications made by its laws are imperfect," Dandridge v. Williams. Just as a policy barring the hiring of methadone users as transit employees does not violate equal protection simply because some methadone users pose no threat to passenger safety, see New York City Transit Authority v. Beazer, and just as a mandatory retirement age of 50 for police officers does not violate equal protection even though it prematurely ends the careers of many policemen over 50 who still have the capacity to do the job, see Massachusetts Bd. of Retirement v. Murgia, Amendment 2 is not constitutionally invalid simply because it could have been drawn more precisely so as to withdraw special antidiscrimination protections only from those of homosexual "orientation" who actually engage in homosexual conduct. As Justice Kennedy wrote, when he was on the Court of Appeals, in a case involving discharge of homosexuals from the Navy: "Nearly any statute which classifies people may be irrational as applied in particular cases. Discharge of the particular plaintiffs before us would be rational, under minimal scrutiny, not because their particular cases present the dangers which justify Navy policy, but instead because the general policy of discharging all homosexuals is rational." Beller v. Middendorf, 632 F.2d 788, 808-809, n.20 (CA9 1980) (citation omitted). . . .

III

The foregoing suffices to establish what the Court's failure to cite any case remotely in point would lead one to suspect: No principle set forth in the Constitution, nor even any imagined by this Court in the past 200 years, prohibits what Colorado has done here. But the case for Colorado is much stronger than that. What it has done is not only unprohibited, but eminently reasonable, with close, congressionally approved precedent in earlier constitutional practice.

First, as to its eminent reasonableness. The Court's opinion contains grim, disapproving hints that Coloradans have been guilty of "animus" or "animosity" toward homosexuality, as though that has been established as Unamerican. Of course it is our moral heritage that one should not hate any human being or class of human beings. But I had thought that one could consider certain conduct reprehensible—murder, for example, or polygamy, or cruelty to animals—and could exhibit even "animus" toward such conduct. Surely that is the only sort of "animus" at issue here: moral disapproval of homosexual conduct, the same sort of moral disapproval that produced the centuries-old criminal laws that we held constitutional in *Bowers.* The Colorado amendment does not, to speak entirely precisely, prohibit giving favored status to people who are homosexuals; they can be favored for many reasons—for example, because they are senior citizens or members of racial minorities. But it prohibits giving them favored status because of their homosexual conduct—that is, it prohibits favored status for homosexuality.

But though Coloradans are, as I say, entitled to be hostile toward homosexual conduct, the fact is that the degree of hostility reflected by Amendment 2 is the smallest conceivable. The Court's portrayal of Coloradans as a society fallen victim to pointless, hate-filled "gay-bashing" is so false as to be comical. Colorado not only is one of the 25 States that have repealed their antisodomy laws, but was among the first to do so. But the society that eliminates criminal punishment for homosexual acts does not necessarily abandon the view that homosexuality is morally wrong and socially harmful; often, abolition simply reflects the view that enforcement of such criminal laws involves unseemly intrusion into the intimate lives of citizens.

There is a problem, however, which arises when criminal sanction of homosexuality is eliminated but moral and social disapprobation of homosexuality is meant to be retained. The Court cannot be unaware of that problem; it is evident in many cities of the country, and occasionally bubbles to the surface of the news, in heated political disputes over such matters as the introduction into local schools of books teaching that homosexuality is an optional and fully acceptable "alternate life style." The problem (a problem, that is, for those who wish to retain social disapprobation of homosexuality) is that, because those who engage in homosexual conduct tend to reside in disproportionate numbers in certain communities, have high disposable income, and of course care about homosexual-rights issues much more ardently than the public at large, they possess political power much greater than their numbers, both locally and statewide. Quite understandably, they devote this political power to achieving not merely a grudging social toleration, but full social acceptance, of homosexuality.

By the time Coloradans were asked to vote on Amendment 2, their exposure to homosexuals' quest for social endorsement was not limited to newspaper accounts of happenings in places such as New York, Los Angeles, San Francisco, and Key West. Three Colorado cities—Aspen, Boulder, and Denver—had enacted ordinances that listed "sexual orientation" as an impermissible ground for discrimination, equating the moral disapproval of homosexual conduct with racial and religious bigotry. The phenomenon had even appeared statewide: the Governor of Colorado had signed an executive order pronouncing that "in the State of Colorado we recognize the diversity in our pluralistic society and strive to bring an end to discrimination in any form," and directing state agency-heads to "ensure non-discrimination" in hiring and promotion based on, among other things, "sexual orientation." I do not mean to be critical of these legislative successes; homosexuals are as entitled to use the legal system for reinforcement of their moral sentiments as are the rest of society. But they are subject to being countered by lawful, democratic countermeasures as well.

That is where Amendment 2 came in. It sought to counter both the geographic concentration and the disproportionate political power of homosexuals by (1) resolving the controversy at the statewide level, and (2) making the election a single-issue contest for both sides. It put directly, to all the citizens of the State, the question: Should homosexuality be given special protection? They answered no. The Court today asserts that this most democratic of procedures is unconstitutional. Lacking any cases to establish that facially absurd proposition, it simply asserts that it must be unconstitutional, because it has never happened before. . . .

What the Court says is even demonstrably false at the constitutional level. The Eighteenth Amendment to the Federal Constitution, for example, deprived those who drank alcohol not only of the power to alter the policy of prohibition locally or through state legislation, but even of the power to alter it through state constitutional amendment or federal legislation. The Establishment Clause of the First Amendment prevents theocrats from having their way by converting their fellow citizens at the local, state, or federal statutory level; as does the Republican Form of Government Clause prevent monarchists.

But there is a much closer analogy, one that involves precisely the effort by the majority of citizens to preserve its view of sexual morality statewide, against the efforts of a geographically concentrated and politically powerful minority to undermine it. The constitutions of the States of Arizona, Idaho, New Mexico, Oklahoma, and Utah to this day contain provisions stating that polygamy is "forever prohibited." Polygamists, and those who have a polygamous "orientation," have been "singled out" by these provisions for much more severe treatment than merely denial of favored status; and that treatment can only be changed by achieving amendment of the state constitutions. The Court's disposition today suggests that these provisions are unconstitutional, and that polygamy must be permitted in these States on a state-legislated, or perhaps even local-option, basis—unless, of course, polygamists for some reason have fewer constitutional rights than homosexuals.

The United States Congress, by the way, required the inclusion of these antipolygamy provisions in the constitutions of Arizona, New Mexico, Oklahoma, and Utah, as a condition of their admission to statehood. (For Arizona, New Mexico, and Utah, moreover, the Enabling Acts required that the antipolygamy provisions be "irrevocable without the consent of the United States and the people of said State"—so that not only were "each of [the] parts" of these States not "open on impartial terms" to polygamists, but even the States as a whole were not; polygamists would have to persuade the whole country to their way of thinking.) [Thus], this "singling out" of the sexual practices of a single group for statewide, democratic vote—so utterly alien to our constitutional system, the Court would have us believe—has not only happened, but has received the explicit approval of the United States Congress.

I cannot say that this Court has explicitly approved any of these state constitutional provisions; but it has approved a territorial statutory provision that went even further, depriving polygamists of the ability even to achieve a constitutional amendment, by depriving them of the power to vote. In

Davis v. Beason, 133 U.S. 333, (1890), Justice Field wrote for a unanimous Court:

> In our judgment, §501 of the Revised Statutes of Idaho Territory, which provides that "no person . . . who is a bigamist or polygamist or who teaches, advises, counsels, or encourages any person or persons to become bigamists or polygamists, or to commit any other crime defined by law, or to enter into what is known as plural or celestial marriage, or who is a member of any order, organization or association which teaches, advises, counsels, or encourages its members or devotees or any other persons to commit the crime of bigamy or polygamy, or any other crime defined by law . . . is permitted to vote at any election, or to hold any position or office of honor, trust, or profit within this Territory," is not open to any constitutional or legal objection.

To the extent, if any, that this opinion permits the imposition of adverse consequences upon mere abstract advocacy of polygamy, it has of course been overruled by later cases. See Brandenburg v. Ohio, 395 U.S. 444 (1969) (per curiam). But the proposition that polygamy can be criminalized, and those engaging in that crime deprived of the vote, remains good law. See Richardson v. Ramirez, 418 U.S. 24, 53, (1974). Beason rejected the argument that "such discrimination is a denial of the equal protection of the laws." Among the Justices joining in that rejection were the two whose views in other cases the Court today treats as equal-protection lodestars—Justice Harlan, who was to proclaim in Plessy v. Ferguson, (dissenting opinion), that the Constitution "neither knows nor tolerates classes among citizens," and Justice Bradley, who had earlier declared that "class legislation . . . [is] obnoxious to the prohibitions of the Fourteenth Amendment," Civil Rights Cases.

This Court cited *Beason* with approval as recently as 1993, in an opinion authored by the same Justice who writes for the Court today. That opinion said: "Adverse impact will not always lead to a finding of impermissible targeting. For example, a social harm may have been a legitimate concern of government for reasons quite apart from discrimination. . . . See, e.g., . . . Davis v. Beason." Church of Lukumi Babalu Aye, Inc. v. Hialeah, 508 U.S. 520, 535, (1993). It remains to be explained how §501 of the Idaho Revised Statutes was not an "impermissible targeting" of polygamists, but (the much more mild) Amendment 2 is an "impermissible targeting" of homosexuals. Has the Court concluded that the perceived social harm of polygamy is a "legitimate concern of government," and the perceived social harm of homosexuality is not?

IV

I strongly suspect that the answer to the last question is yes, which leads me to the last point I wish to make: The Court today, announcing that

Amendment 2 "defies . . . conventional [constitutional] inquiry," and "confounds [the] normal process of judicial review," employs a constitutional theory heretofore unknown to frustrate Colorado's reasonable effort to preserve traditional American moral values. The Court's stern disapproval of "animosity" towards homosexuality might be compared with what an earlier Court (including the revered Justices Harlan and Bradley) said in Murphy v. Ramsey, 114 U.S. 15 (1885), rejecting a constitutional challenge to a United States statute that denied the franchise in federal territories to those who engaged in polygamous cohabitation:

> Certainly no legislation can be supposed more wholesome and necessary in the founding of a free, self-governing commonwealth, fit to take rank as one of the co-ordinate States of the Union, than that which seeks to establish it on the basis of the idea of the family, as consisting in and springing from the union for life of one man and one woman in the holy estate of matrimony; the sure foundation of all that is stable and noble in our civilization; the best guaranty of that reverent morality which is the source of all beneficent progress in social and political improvement.

I would not myself indulge in such official praise for heterosexual monogamy, because I think it no business of the courts (as opposed to the political branches) to take sides in this culture war.

But the Court today has done so, not only by inventing a novel and extravagant constitutional doctrine to take the victory away from traditional forces, but even by verbally disparaging as bigotry adherence to traditional attitudes. To suggest, for example, that this constitutional amendment springs from nothing more than "'a bare . . . desire to harm a politically unpopular group'" is nothing short of insulting. (It is also nothing short of preposterous to call "politically unpopular" a group which enjoys enormous influence in American media and politics, and which, as the trial court here noted, though composing no more than 4% of the population had the support of 46% of the voters on Amendment 2.

When the Court takes sides in the culture wars, it tends to be with the knights rather than the villeins—and more specifically with the Templars, reflecting the views and values of the lawyer class from which the Court's Members are drawn. How that class feels about homosexuality will be evident to anyone who wishes to interview job applicants at virtually any of the Nation's law schools. The interviewer may refuse to offer a job because the applicant is a Republican; because he is an adulterer; because he went to the wrong prep school or belongs to the wrong country club; because he eats snails; because he is a womanizer; because she wears real-animal fur; or even because he hates the Chicago Cubs. But if the interviewer should wish not to be an associate or partner of an applicant because he disapproves of the applicant's homosexuality, then he will have violated the pledge which the Association of American Law Schools requires all its member-schools to exact from job interviewers: "assurance of the employer's willingness" to hire homosexuals. This law-school view of what "prejudices" must be stamped out may be contrasted with the more plebeian attitudes that apparently still prevail in the United States Congress, which has been unresponsive to repeated attempts to extend to homosexuals the protections of federal civil rights laws, and which took the pains to exclude them specifically from the Americans With Disabilities Act of 1990.

Today's opinion has no foundation in American constitutional law, and barely pretends to. The people of Colorado have adopted an entirely reasonable provision which does not even disfavor homosexuals in any substantive sense, but merely denies them preferential treatment. Amendment 2 is designed to prevent piecemeal deterioration of the sexual morality favored by a majority of Coloradans, and is not only an appropriate means to that legitimate end, but a means that Americans have employed before. Striking it down is an act, not of judicial judgment, but of political will. I dissent.

Note: The Meaning of Romer

1. *Rational basis review?* The Court asserts that it is utilizing rational basis review to invalidate Amendment 2. Is this claim plausible? Recall Reed v. Reed, page 699 of the main volume, where the Court inaugurated its modern encounter with gender discrimination by purporting to utilize rationale-basis review to invalidate gender-specific laws. Only later did the Court acknowledge that it was utilizing heightened scrutiny. See Craig v. Boren, at page 703 of the main volume. Does *Romer* mark the beginning of an analogous transformation of the Court's jurisprudence regarding sexual preference? If so, what institutional interests are served by insisting on rational-basis review at the beginning of this process?

Note that Amendment 2 was unusually broad in scope. Unlike state constitutional provisions that simply outlaw certain practices, such as polygamy, or the "don't ask/don't tell" policy, which disadvantages homosexuals in a particular context, this provision deprived a class of citizens of access to *any* protection against discrimination, regardless of context, on the basis of a single trait. Even if the denial of protection to homosexuals is rational in *some* contexts, might not the general denial of such protection *regardless of context* be irrational?

2. *Baselines again.* The Court claims that its decision guarantees for homosexuals only "equal" and not "special protection. This is so, the Court asserts, because under modern conditions, the baseline is a general right to be free from discrimination. Protections against discrimination are "taken for granted by most people either because they already have them or do

not need them; these are protections against exclusion from an almost limitless number of transactions and endeavors that constitute ordinary civic life in a free society." Suppose Colorado had never enacted Amendment 2, but had simply failed to enact measures protecting homosexuals from discrimination. Does it follow from the Court's analysis that a state acts "irrationally" and therefore violates the Constitution if it provides general protection against discrimination for a wide range of groups but fails to provide such protection for gays? Is this position consistent with Washington v. Davis?

3. *The future of* Bowers. The Court asserts that Amendment 2 raises "the inevitable inference that the disadvantage imposed is born of animosity toward the class of persons affected" and relies on *Moreno* for the proposition that "[if] the constitutional conception of 'equal protection of the laws' means anything, it must at the very least mean that a bare . . . desire to harm a politically unpopular group cannot constitute a legitimate governmental interest." Can this argument against Amendment 2 be squared with the Court's holding in *Bowers* that moral opposition to homosexuality is a sufficiently strong government interest to justify criminalization of homosexual sodomy? Note that the Court fails to cite *Bowers*, although the decision is surely at least tangentially relevant to the Court's analysis. What message does this failure send?

Does it follow from the government's ability to criminalize certain activity that any other disadvantage the government imposes on those who engage in it is automatically permissible under the equal protection clause? Could the government deny a driver's license to a person caught smoking cigarettes?

4. *Justice Scalia's dissent.* What is the meaning of the first sentence of Justice Scalia's opinion? "Kulturkampf" is the German word for "culture war." The term refers to the effort by the German government in the late 19th century, under the leadership of Count Bismarck, to reduce the influence of the Roman Catholic Church. Among other things, Bismarck insisted that the state train and license priests and imprisoned priests and bishops who disobeyed his orders. Consider the possibility that our Constitution outlaws state-supported "Kulturkampfs" and that Amendment 2 violated the Constitution precisely because it formed part of an official "culture war" against a particular subsection of the population. Note that the majority and dissenting opinions each accuse the other of departing from a position of state neutrality in this conflict. The majority disclaims any effort to give homosexuals "special" rights and claims that Colorado has failed to treat them "equally." The dissent, in turn, accuses the majority of siding with homosexuals against their adversaries. What does state neutrality mean in this context? Is neutrality a desirable or constitutionally required objective?

Chapter Six

Implied Fundamental Rights

F. MODERN SUBSTANTIVE DUE PROCESS: PRIVACY, PERSONHOOD, AND FAMILY

Page 892. Before "c. Denial of 'Access to the Ballot,'" add the following:

BUSH v. VERA

116 S. Ct. — (1996)

JUSTICE O'CONNOR announced the judgment of the Court and delivered an opinion, in which THE CHIEF JUSTICE and JUSTICE KENNEDY join.

This is the latest in a series of appeals involving racial gerrymandering challenges to state redistricting efforts in the wake of the 1990 census. That census revealed a population increase, largely in urban minority populations, that entitled Texas to three additional congressional seats. In response, and with a view to complying with the Voting Rights Act of 1965 (VRA), the Texas Legislature promulgated a redistricting plan that, among other things: created District 30, a new majority-African-American district in Dallas County; created District 29, a new majority-Hispanic district in and around Houston in Harris County; and reconfigured District 18, which is adjacent to District 29, to make it a majority-African-American district. The Department of Justice precleared that plan under VRA §5 in 1991, and it was used in the 1992 congressional elections.

The plaintiffs, six Texas voters, challenged the plan, alleging that 24 of Texas' 30 congressional districts constitute racial gerrymanders in violation of the Fourteenth Amendment. The three-judge United States District Court for the Southern District of Texas held Districts 18, 29, and 30 unconstitutional. . . . The Governor of Texas, private intervenors, and the United States (as intervenor) now appeal. Finding that, under this Court's decisions in *Shaw I* and *Miller*, the district lines at issue are subject to strict scrutiny, and that they are not narrowly tailored to serve a compelling state interest, we affirm. . . .

II

Issue

We must now determine whether those districts are subject to strict scrutiny. Our precedents have used a variety of formulations to describe the threshold for the application of strict scrutiny. . . .

Strict scrutiny does not apply merely because redistricting is performed with consciousness of race. Nor does it apply to all cases of intentional creation of majority-minority districts. Electoral district lines are "facially race neutral," so a more searching inquiry is necessary before strict scrutiny can be found applicable in redistricting cases than in cases of "classifications based explicitly on race." For strict scrutiny to apply, the plaintiffs must prove that other, legitimate districting principles were "subordinated" to race. By that, we mean that race must be "the predominant factor motivating the legislature's [redistricting] decision." We thus differ from Justice Thomas, who would apparently hold that it suffices that racial considerations be a motivation for the drawing of a majority-minority district.

The present case is a mixed motive case. The appellants concede that one of Texas' goals in creating the three districts at issue was to produce majority-minority districts, but they also cite evidence that other goals, particularly incumbency protection (including protection of "functional incumbents," i.e., sitting members of the Texas Legislature who had declared an intention to run for open congressional seats), also played a role in the drawing of the district lines. [A] careful review is, therefore, necessary to determine whether these districts are subject to strict scrutiny. But review of the District Court's findings of primary fact and the record convinces us that the District Court's determination that race was the "predominant factor" in the drawing of each of the districts must be sustained.

We begin with general findings and evidence regarding the redistricting plan's respect for traditional districting principles, the legislators' expressed motivations, and the methods used in the redistricting process. The District Court began its analysis by rejecting the factual basis for appellants' claim that Texas' challenged "districts cannot be unconstitutionally bizarre in shape because Texas does not have and never has used traditional redistricting principles such as natural geographical boundaries, contiguity, compactness, and conformity to political subdivisions." The court instead found that "generally, Texas has not intentionally disregarded traditional districting criteria," and that only one pre-1991 congressional district in Texas was comparable in its irregularity and noncompactness to the three challenged districts. The court also noted that "compactness as measured by an 'eyeball' approach was much less important," in the 1991 plan, than in its predecessor, the 1980 Texas congressional districting plan, and that districts were especially irregular in shape in the Dallas and Harris County areas where the challenged districts are located.

These findings comport with the conclusions of an instructive study that attempted to determine the relative compactness of districts nationwide in objective, numerical terms. That study gave Texas' 1980 districting plan a roughly average score for the compactness and regularity of its district shapes, but ranked its 1991 plan among the worst in the Nation. See Pildes & Niemi, Expressive Harms, "Bizarre Districts," and Voting Rights: Evaluating Election-District Appearances After Shaw v. Reno, 92 Mich. L. Rev. 483, 571-573, table 6 (1993). The same study ranked Districts 18, 29, and 30 among the 28 least regular congressional districts nationwide. . . .

The District Court also found substantial direct evidence of the legislature's racial motivations. . . .

The means that Texas used to make its redistricting decisions provides further evidence of the importance of race. The primary tool used in drawing district lines was a computer program called "REDAPPL." REDAPPL permitted redistricters to manipulate district lines on computer maps, on which racial and other socioeconomic data were superimposed. At each change in configuration of the district lines being drafted, REDAPPL displayed updated racial composition statistics for the district as drawn. REDAPPL contained racial data at the block-by-block level, whereas other data, such as party registration and past voting statistics, were only available at the level of voter tabulation districts (which approximate election precincts). The availability and use of block-by-block racial data was unprecedented; before the 1990 census, data were not broken down beyond the census tract level. By providing uniquely detailed racial data, REDAPPL enabled districters to make more intricate refinements on the basis of race than on the basis of other demographic information. . . .

These findings—that the State substantially neglected traditional districting criteria such as compactness, that it was committed from the outset to creating majority-minority districts, and that it manipulated district lines to exploit unprecedentedly detailed racial data—together weigh in favor of the application of strict scrutiny. We do not hold that any one of these factors is independently sufficient to require strict scrutiny. The Constitution does not mandate regularity of district shape, and the neglect of traditional districting criteria is merely necessary, not sufficient. For strict scrutiny to apply, traditional districting criteria must be subordinated to race. Nor, as we have emphasized, is the decision to create a majority-minority district objectionable in and of itself. . . .

Several factors other than race were at work in the drawing of the districts. Traditional districting criteria were not entirely neglected. [The] District Court found that incumbency protection influenced the redistricting plan to an unprecedented extent. . . .

Strict scrutiny would not be appropriate if race-neutral, traditional districting considerations predominated over racial ones. We have not subjected political gerrymandering to strict scrutiny. [Because] it is clear that race was not the only factor that motivated the legislature to draw irregular district lines, we must scrutinize each challenged district to determine whether the District Court's conclusion that race predominated over legitimate districting considerations, including incumbency, can be sustained.

A . . .

Appellants do not deny that District 30 shows substantial disregard for the traditional districting principles of compactness and regularity, or that the redistricters pursued unwaveringly the objective of creating a majority-African-American district. But they argue that its bizarre shape is explained by efforts to unite communities of interest in a single district and, especially, to protect incumbents. . . .

Here, the District Court had ample bases on which to conclude both that racially motivated gerrymandering had a qualitatively greater influence on the drawing of district lines than politically motivated gerrymandering, and that political gerrymandering was accomplished in large part by the use of race as a proxy. . . .

[Most] significantly, the objective evidence provided by the district plans and demographic maps suggests strongly the predominance of race. Given that the districting software used by the State provided only racial data at the block-by-block level, the fact that District 30, unlike Johnson's original proposal, splits voter tabulation districts and even individual streets in many places, suggests that racial criteria predominated over other districting criteria in determining the district's boundaries. And, despite the strong correlation between race and political affiliation, the maps reveal that political considerations were subordinated to racial classification in the drawing of many of the most extreme and bizarre district lines.

B . . .

District 18's population is 51% African-American and 15% Hispanic. It "has some of the most irregular boundaries of any congressional district in the country[,] . . . boundaries that squiggle north toward Intercontinental Airport and northwest out radial highways, then spurt south on one side toward the port and on the other toward the Astrodome. Its "many narrow corridors, wings, or fingers . . . reach out to enclose black voters, while excluding nearby Hispanic residents."

District 29 has a 61% Hispanic and 10% African-American population. It resembles

> a sacred Mayan bird, with its body running eastward along the Ship Channel from downtown Houston until the tail terminates in Baytown. Spindly legs reach south to Hobby Airport, while the plumed head rises northward almost to Intercontinental. In the western extremity of the district, an open beak appears to be searching for worms in Spring Branch. Here and there, ruffled feathers jut out at odd angles.

Not only are the shapes of the districts bizarre; they also exhibit utter disregard of city limits, local election precincts, and voter tabulation district lines. . . .

As with District 30, appellants adduced evidence that incumbency protection played a role in determining the bizarre district lines. The District Court found that one constraint on the shape of District 29 was the rival ambitions of its two "functional incumbents," who distorted its boundaries in an effort to include larger areas of their existing state legislative constituencies. But the District Court's findings amply demonstrate that such influences were overwhelmed in the determination of the districts' bizarre shapes by the State's efforts to maximize racial divisions. . . .

III

Having concluded that strict scrutiny applies, we must determine whether the racial classifications embodied in any of the three districts are narrowly tailored to further a compelling state interest. Appellants point to three compelling interests: the interest in avoiding liability under the "results" test of VRA §2(b), the interest in remedying past and present racial discrimination, and the "nonretrogression" principle of VRA §5 (for District 18 only). . . .

A

Section 2(a) of the VRA prohibits the imposition of any electoral practice or procedure that "results in a denial or abridgement of the right of any citizen . . . to vote on account of race or color." In 1982, Congress amended the VRA by changing the language of §2(a) and adding §2(b), which provides a "results" test for violation of §2(a). A violation exists if,

> based on the totality of circumstances, it is shown that the political processes leading to nomination or election in the State or political subdivision are not equally open to participation by members of a class of citizens protected by subsection (a) of this section in that its members have less opportunity than other members of the electorate to participate in the political process and to elect representatives of their choice. 42 U.S.C. §1973(b).

Appellants contend that creation of each of the three majority-minority districts at issue was justified by Texas' compelling state interest in complying with this results test.

As we have done in each of our previous cases in which this argument has been raised as a defense to charges of racial gerrymandering, we assume without deciding that compliance with the results test [can] be a compelling state interest. We also reaffirm that the "narrow tailoring" requirement of strict scrutiny allows the States a limited degree of leeway in furthering such interests. If the State has a "strong basis in evidence," for concluding that creation of a majority-minority district is reasonably necessary to comply with §2, and the districting that is based on race "substantially addresses the §2 violation," it satisfies strict scrutiny. We thus reject, as impossibly stringent, the District Court's view of the narrow tailoring requirement, that "a district must have the least possible amount of irregularity in shape, making allowances for traditional districting criteria.". . .

We assume, without deciding, that the State had a "strong basis in evidence" for finding the second and third threshold conditions for §2 liability to be present. We have, however, already found that all three districts are bizarrely shaped and far from compact, and that those characteristics are predominantly attributable to gerrymandering that was racially motivated and/or achieved by the use of race as a proxy. . . .

These characteristics defeat any claim that the districts are narrowly tailored to serve the State's interest in avoiding liability under §2, because §2 does not require a State to create, on predominantly racial lines, a district that is not "reasonably compact." . . .

B

The United States and the State next contend that the district lines at issue are justified by the State's compelling interest in "ameliorating the effects of racially polarized voting attributable to past and present racial discrimination." In support of that contention, they cite Texas' long history of discrimination against minorities in electoral processes, stretching from the Reconstruction to modern times, including violations of the Constitution and of the VRA. Appellants attempt to link that history to evidence that in recent elections in majority-minority districts, "Anglos usually bloc voted against" Hispanic and African-American candidates.

A State's interest in remedying discrimination is compelling when two conditions are satisfied. First, the discrimination that the State seeks to remedy must be specific, "identified discrimination"; second, the State "must have had a 'strong basis in evidence' to conclude that remedial action was necessary, 'before it embarks on an affirmative action program.' " Here, the only current problem that appellants cite as in need of remediation is alleged vote dilution as a consequence of racial bloc voting, the same concern that underlies their VRA §2 compliance defense, which we have assumed to be valid for purposes of this opinion. We have indicated that such problems will not justify race-based districting unless "the State employs sound districting principles, and . . . the affected racial group's residential patterns afford the opportunity of creating districts in which they will be in the majority." Once that standard is applied, our agreement with the District Court's finding that these districts are not narrowly tailored to comply with §2 forecloses this line of defense.

C

The final contention offered by the State and private appellants is that creation of District 18 (only) was justified by a compelling state interest in complying with VRA §5. We have made clear that §5 has a limited substantive goal: "'to insure that no voting-procedure changes would be made that would lead to a retrogression in the position of racial minorities with respect to their effective exercise of the electoral franchise.'" Appellants contend that this "nonretrogression" principle is implicated because Harris County had, for two decades, contained a congressional district in which African-American voters had succeeded in selecting representatives of their choice, all of whom were African-Americans.

The problem with the State's argument is that it seeks to justify not maintenance, but substantial augmentation, of the African-American population percentage in District 18. . . .

IV . . .

This Court has now rendered decisions after plenary consideration in five cases applying the *Shaw I* doctrine (*Shaw I, Miller, Hays, Shaw II,* and this case). The dissenters would have us abandon those precedents, suggesting that fundamental concerns relating to the judicial role are at stake. While we agree that those concerns are implicated here, we believe they point the other way. Our legitimacy requires, above all, that we adhere to stare decisis, especially in such sensitive political contexts as the present, where partisan controversy abounds. Legislators and district courts nationwide have modified their practices—or, rather, reembraced the traditional districting practices that were almost universally followed before the 1990 census—in response to *Shaw I.* Those practices and our precedents, which acknowledge voters as more than mere racial statistics, play an important role in defining the political identity of the American voter. Our Fourteenth Amendment jurisprudence evinces a commitment to eliminate unnecessary and excessive governmental use and reinforcement of racial stereotypes. We decline to retreat from that commitment today.

The judgment of the District Court is
Affirmed.

JUSTICE O'CONNOR, concurring.

I write separately to express my view on two points. First, compliance with the results test of §2 of the Voting Rights Act (VRA) is a compelling state interest. Second, that test can co-exist in principle and in practice with Shaw v. Reno and its progeny, as elaborated in today's opinions. . . .

JUSTICE KENNEDY, concurring.

I join the plurality opinion, but the statements in Part II of the opinion that strict scrutiny would not apply to all cases of intentional creation of majority-minority districts require comment. Those statements are unnecessary to our decision, for strict scrutiny applies here. I do not consider these dicta to commit me to any position on the question whether race is predominant whenever a State, in redistricting, foreordains that one race be the majority in a certain number of districts or in a certain part of the State. In my view, we would no doubt apply strict scrutiny if a State decreed that certain districts had to be at least 50 percent white, and our analysis should be no different if the State so favors minority races. . . .

JUSTICE THOMAS, with whom JUSTICE SCALIA joins, concurring in the judgment.

In my view, application of strict scrutiny in this case was never a close question. I cannot agree with Justice O'Connor's assertion that strict scrutiny is not invoked by the intentional creation of majority-minority districts. . . .

Strict scrutiny applies to all governmental classifications based on race, and we have expressly held that there is no exception for race-based redistricting. . . .

I am willing to assume without deciding that the State has asserted a compelling state interest. Given that assumption, I agree that the State's redistricting attempts were not narrowly tailored to achieve its asserted interest. I concur in the judgment.

JUSTICE STEVENS, with whom JUSTICE GINSBURG and JUSTICE BREYER join, dissenting.

The 1990 census revealed that Texas' population had grown, over the past decade, almost twice as fast as the population of the country as a whole. As a result, Texas was entitled to elect three additional Representatives to the United States Congress, enlarging its delegation from 27 to 30. Because Texas' growth was concentrated in South Texas and the cities of Dallas and Houston, the state legislature concluded that the new congressional districts should be carved out of existing districts in those areas. The consequences of the political battle that produced the new map are some of the most oddly shaped congressional districts in the United States.

Today, the Court strikes down three of Texas' majority- minority districts, concluding, inter alia, that their odd shapes reveal that the State impermissibly relied on predominantly racial reasons when it drew the districts as it did. For two reasons, I believe that the Court errs in striking down those districts.

First, I believe that the Court has misapplied its own tests for racial gerrymandering, both by applying strict scrutiny to all three of these districts, and then by concluding that none can meet that scrutiny. In asking whether strict scrutiny should apply, the Court improperly ignores the "complex interplay" of political and geographical considerations that went into the creation of Texas' new congressional districts, and focuses exclusively on the role that race played in the State's decisions to adjust the shape of its districts. A quick comparison of the unconstitutional majority-minority districts with three equally bizarre majority-Anglo districts demonstrates that race was not necessarily the predominant factor contorting the district lines. I would follow the fair implications of the District Court's findings and conclude that Texas' entire map is a political, not a racial, gerrymander. . . .

Even if strict scrutiny applies, I would find these districts constitutional, for each considers race only to the extent necessary to comply with the State's responsibilities under the Voting Rights Act while achieving other race-neutral political and geographical requirements. The plurality's finding to the contrary unnecessarily restricts the ability of States to conform their behavior to the Voting Rights Act while simultaneously complying with other race-neutral goals.

Second, even if I concluded that these districts failed an appropriate application of this still-developing law to appropriately read facts, I would not uphold the District Court decision. The decisions issued today serve merely to reinforce my conviction that the Court has, with its "analytically distinct" jurisprudence of racial gerrymandering, struck out into a jurisprudential wilderness that lacks a definable constitutional core and threatens to create harms more significant than any suffered by the individual plaintiffs challenging these districts. . . .

II . . .

The conclusion that race-conscious districting should not always be subject to strict scrutiny merely recognizes that our equal protection jurisprudence can sometimes mislead us with its rigid characterization of suspect classes and levels of scrutiny. As I have previously noted, all equal protection jurisprudence might be described as a form of rational basis scrutiny; we apply "strict scrutiny" more to describe the likelihood of success than the character of the test to be applied. Because race has rarely been a legitimate basis for state classifications, and more typically an irrational and invidious ground for discrimination, a "virtually automatic invalidation of racial classifications" has been the natural result of the application of our equal protection jurisprudence. In certain circumstances, however, when the state action (i) has neither the intent nor effect of harming any particular group, (ii) is not designed to give effect to irrational prejudices held by its citizens but to break them down, and (iii) uses race as a classification because race is "relevant" to the benign goal of the classification, we need not view the action with the typically fatal skepticism that we have used to strike down the most pernicious forms of state behavior. [While] any racial classification may risk some stereotyping, the risk of true "discrimination" in this case is extremely tenuous in light of the remedial purpose the classification is intended to achieve and the long history of resistance to giving minorities a full voice in the political process. Given the balancing of subtle harms and strong remedies—a balancing best left to the political process, not to our own well-developed but rigid jurisprudence—the plurality reasonably concludes that race-conscious redistricting is not always a form of "discrimination" to which we should direct our most skeptical eye.

III

While the Court has agreed that race can, to a point, govern the drawing of district lines, it nonetheless suggests that at a certain point, when the State uses race "too much," illegitimate racial stereotypes threaten to overrun and contaminate an otherwise legitimate redistricting process. . . .

IV . . .

The political, rather than the racial, nature of District 30's gerrymander is even more starkly highlighted by comparing it with the districts struck down in *Shaw II* and *Miller.* District 30's black population is, for instance, far more concentrated than the minority population in North Carolina's District 12. And in *Miller*, the Court made it clear that the odd shape of Georgia's Eleventh District was the result of a conscious effort to increase its proportion of minority populations: It was, the Court found, "'exceedingly obvious' from the shape of the Eleventh District, together with the racial demographics, that the drawing of narrow land bridges to incorporate within the District outlying appendages containing nearly 80% of the district's total black population was a deliberate attempt to bring black populations into the district."

District 30 is the precise demographic converse of the district struck down in Miller. District 30, for example, has a compact core in South Dallas which contains 50% of the district population and nearly 70% of the district's total black population. Unlike the appendages to Georgia's District 11, the tentacles stretching north and west from District 30 add progressively less in the way of population, and, more important for purposes of this inquiry, they actually reduce the proportional share of minorities in the district. . . .

In sum, a fair analysis of the shape of District 30, like the equally bizarre shape of District 6, belies the notion that its shape was determined by racial considerations. . . .

Perhaps conscious that noncompact congressional districts are the rule rather than the exception in Texas, the plurality suggests, that the real key is the direct evidence, particularly in the form of Texas' §5 Voting Rights Act submissions and the person of then-State Senator Johnson, that the State expressed an intent to create these districts with a given "minimum percentage of the favored minority." Even if it were appropriate to rest this test of dominance on an examination of the subjective motivation of individual legislators, or on testimony given in a legal proceeding designed to prove a conflicting conclusion, this information does little more than confirm that the State believed it necessary to comply with the Voting Rights Act. . . .

In an effort to provide a definitive explanation for the odd shape of the district, the State emphasized two factors: The presence of communities of interest tying together the populations of the district, and the role of incumbency protection. The District Court and the plurality improperly dismissed these considerations as ultimately irrelevant to the shape of the districts.

[The] appellants presented testimony that the districts were drawn to align with certain communities of interest, such as land use, family demographics, and transportation corridors. . . .

Nonracial Factors: Incumbency

The plurality admits that the appellants "present a . . . substantial case for their claim that incumbency protection rivalled race in determining the district's shape.". . .

Race as a Proxy

Faced with all this evidence that politics, not race, was the predominant factor shaping the district lines, the plurality ultimately makes little effort to contradict appellants' assertions that incumbency protection was far more important in the placement of District 30's lines than race. . . .

I note that in most contexts racial classifications are invidious because they are irrational. For example, it is irrational to assume that a person is not qualified to vote or to serve as a juror simply because she has brown hair or brown skin. It is neither irrational, nor invidious, however, to assume that a black resident of a particular community is a Democrat if reliable statistical evidence discloses that 97% of the blacks in that community vote in Democratic primary elections. For that reason, the fact that the architects of the Texas plan sometimes appear to have used racial data as a proxy for making political judgments seems to me to be no more "unjustified," and to have no more constitutional significance, than an assumption that wealthy suburbanites, whether black or white, are more likely to be Republicans than communists. Requiring the State to ignore the association between race and party affiliation would be no more logical, and potentially as harmful, as it would be to prohibit the Public Health Service from targeting African-American communities in an effort to increase awareness regarding sickle-cell anemia.

Despite all the efforts by the plurality and the District Court, then, the evidence demonstrates that race was not, in all likelihood, the "predominant" goal leading to the creation of District 30. The most reasonable interpretation of the record evidence instead demonstrates that political considerations were. In accord with the presumption against interference with a legislature's consideration of complex and competing factors, I would conclude that the configuration of District 30 does not require strict scrutiny.

VI

I cannot profess to know how the Court's developing jurisprudence of racial gerrymandering will alter the political and racial landscape in this Nation—although it certainly will alter that landscape. As the Court's law in this area has developed, it has become ever more apparent to me that the Court's approach to these cases creates certain perverse incentives and (I presume) unanticipated effects that serve to highlight the essentially unknown territory into which it strides. Because I believe that the social and political risks created by the Court's decisions are not required by the Constitution, my first choice would be to avoid the preceding analysis altogether, and leave these considerations to the political branches of our Government.

The first unintended outcome of the legal reasoning in *Shaw II* and *Bush* is the very result that those decisions seek to avoid: The predominance of race in the districting process, over all other principles of importance. Given the Court's unwillingness to recognize the role that race-neutral districting principles played in the creation of the bizarrely shaped districts in both this case and *Shaw II*, it now seems clear that the only way that a State can both create a majority-minority district and avoid a racial gerrymander is by drawing, "without much conscious thought," and within the "limited degree of leeway" granted by the Court, the precise compact district that a court would impose in a successful §2 challenge. After the Court's decisions today, therefore, minority voters can make up a majority only in compact districts, whether intentionally or accidentally drawn, while white voters can be placed into districts as bizarre as the State desires.

The great irony, of course, is that by requiring the State to place the majority-minority district in a particular place and with a particular shape, the district may stand out as a stark, placid island in a sea of oddly shaped majority-white neighbors. . . .

Regardless of the route taken by the States, the Court has guaranteed that federal courts will have a hand—and perhaps the only hand—in the "abrasive task of drawing district lines." Given the uniquely political nature of the redistricting process, I fear the impact this new role will have on the public's perception of the impartiality of the federal judiciary. . . .

JUSTICE SOUTER, with whom JUSTICE GINSBURG and JUSTICE BREYER join, dissenting.

When the Court devises a new cause of action to enforce a constitutional provision, it ought to identify an injury distinguishable from the consequences of concededly constitutional conduct, and it should describe the elements necessary and sufficient to make out such a claim. Nothing less can give notice to those whose conduct may give rise to liability or provide standards for courts charged with enforcing the Constitution. . . .

Today's opinions do little to solve *Shaw*'s puzzles or return districting responsibility to the States. To say this is not to denigrate the importance of Justice O'Connor's position in her separate opinion that compliance with §2 of the Voting Rights Act is a compelling state interest; her statement takes a very significant step toward alleviating apprehension that *Shaw* is at odds with the Voting Rights Act. It is still true, however, that the combined plurality, minority, and Court opinions do not ultimately leave the law dealing with a Shaw claim appreciably clearer or more manageable than *Shaw I* itself did. And to the extent that some clarity follows from the knowledge that race may be considered when reasonably necessary to conform to the Voting Rights Act, today's opinions raise the specter that this ostensible progress may come with a heavy constitutional price. The price of *Shaw I*, indeed, may turn out to be the practical elimination of a State's discretion to apply traditional districting principles, widely accepted in States without racial districting issues as well as in States confronting them.

As the flaws of *Shaw I* persist, and as the burdens placed on the States and the courts by *Shaw* litigation loom larger with the approach of a new census and a new round of redistricting, the Court has to recognize that *Shaw*'s problems result from a basic misconception about the relation between race and districting principles, a mistake that no amount of case-by-case tinkering can eliminate. There is, therefore, no reason for confidence that the Court will eventually bring much order out of the confusion created by *Shaw I*, and because it has not, in any case, done so yet, I respectfully dissent. . . .

SHAW v. HUNT

116 S. Ct. — (1996)

CHIEF JUSTICE REHNQUIST delivered the opinion of the Court. . . .

[Racial] classifications are antithetical to the Fourteenth Amendment, whose "central purpose" was "to eliminate racial discrimination emanating from official sources in the States." While appreciating that a racial classification causes "fundamental injury" to the "individual rights of a person," we have recognized that, under certain circumstances, drawing racial distinctions is permissible where a governmental body is pursuing a "compelling state interest." A State, however, is constrained in how it may pursue that end: "The means chosen to accomplish the State's asserted purpose must be specifically and narrowly framed to accomplish that purpose." North Carolina, therefore, must show not only that its redistricting plan was in pursuit of a compelling state interest, but also that "its districting legislation is narrowly tailored to achieve [that] compelling interest.

Appellees point to three separate compelling interests to sustain District 12: to eradicate the effects of past and present discrimination; to comply with §5 of the Voting Rights Act; and to comply with §2 of that Act. We address each in turn.

A State's interest in remedying the effects of past or present racial discrimination may in the proper case justify a government's use of racial distinctions. For that interest to rise to the level of a compelling state interest, it must satisfy two conditions. First, the discrimination must be "'identified discrimination.'" "While the States and their subdivisions may take remedial action when they possess evidence" of past or present discrimination, "they must identify that discrimination, public or private, with some specificity before they may use race-conscious relief." A generalized assertion of past discrimination in a particular industry or region is not adequate because it "provides no guidance for a legislative body to determine the precise scope of the injury it seeks to remedy." Accordingly, an effort to alleviate the effects of societal discrimination is not a compelling interest. Second, the institution that makes the racial distinction must have had a "strong basis in evidence" to conclude that remedial action was necessary, "before it embarks on an affirmative-action program."

In this case, the District Court found that an interest in ameliorating past discrimination did not actually precipitate the use of race in the redistricting plan. While some legislators invoked the State's history of discrimination as an argument for creating a second majority-black district, the court found that these members did not have enough voting power to have caused the creation of the second district on that basis alone.

[And] there is little to suggest that the legislature considered the historical events and social-science data that the reports recount, beyond what individual members may have recalled from personal experience. We certainly cannot say on the basis of these reports that the District Court's findings on this point were clearly erroneous.

Appellees devote most of their efforts to arguing that the race-based redistricting was constitutionally justified by the State's duty to comply with the Voting Rights Act. [In] *Miller*, we expressly left open the question whether under the proper circumstances compliance with the Voting Rights Act, on its own, could be a compelling interest. Here once again we do not reach that question because we find that creating an additional majority-black district was not required under a correct reading of § 5 and that District 12, as drawn, is not a remedy narrowly tailored to the State's professed interest in avoiding § 2liability. . . .

For the foregoing reasons, the judgment of the District Court is Reversed.

JUSTICE STEVENS, with whom JUSTICE GINSBURG and JUSTICE BREYER join as to Parts II-V, dissenting. . . .

II

[*Shaw I*] is entirely consistent with our holdings that race-based districting which respects traditional districting principles does not give rise to constitutional suspicion. As the District Court noted, Shaw I expressly reserved the question whether "'the intentional creation of majority-minority districts, without more,' always gives rise to an equal protection claim." *Shaw I* held only that an equal protection claim could lie as a result of allegations suggesting that the State's districting was "so extremely irregular on its face that it rationally can be viewed only as an effort to segregate the races for purposes of voting, without regard for traditional districting principles[.]"

Moreover, *Miller* belies the conclusion that strict scrutiny must apply to all deliberate attempts to draw majority-minority districts if the Equal Protection Clause is to provide any practical limitation on a State's power to engage in race-based districting. Although Georgia argued that it had complied with traditional districting principles, the *Miller* majority had little difficulty concluding that the State's race-neutral explanations were implausible. Thus, *Miller* demonstrates that although States may avoid strict scrutiny by complying with traditional districting principles, they may not do so by proffering pretextual, race-neutral explanations for their maps.

The notion that conscientious federal judges will be able to distinguish race-neutral explanations from pretextual ones is hardly foreign to our race discrimination jurisprudence. In a variety of contexts, from employment to juror selection, we have required plaintiffs to demonstrate not only that a defendant's action could be understood as impermissibly race-based, but also that the defendant's assertedly race-neutral explanation for that action was in fact a pretext for racial discrimination. . . .

North Carolina's admission reveals that it intended to create a second majority-minority district. That says nothing about whether it subordinated traditional districting principles in drawing District 12. States which conclude that federal law requires majority-minority districts have little choice but to give "overriding" weight to that concern. . . .

District 12's noncompact appearance also fails to show that North Carolina engaged in suspect race-based districting. There is no federal statutory or constitutional requirement that state electoral boundaries conform to any particular ideal of geographic compactness. . . .

There is a more fundamental flaw in the majority's conclusion that racial concerns predominantly explain the creation of District 12. The evidence of shape and intent relied on by the majority cannot overcome the basic fact that North Carolina did not have to draw Districts 1 and 12 in order to comply with the Justice Department's finding that federal law required the creation of two majority-minority districts. That goal could have been more straightforwardly accomplished by simply adopting the Attorney General's recommendation to draw a geographically compact district in the southeastern portion of the State in addition to the majority-minority district that had already been drawn in the northeastern and Piedmont regions.

That the legislature chose to draw Districts 1 and 12 instead surely suggests that something more than the desire to create a majority-minority district took precedence. For that reason, this case would seem to present a version of the very hypothetical that the principal opinion in Bush suggests should pose no constitutional problem—"an otherwise compact majority-minority district that is misshapen by nonracial, political manipulation." . . .

A deliberate effort to consolidate urban voters in one district and rural voters in another also explains District 12's highly irregular shape. Before District 12 had been drawn, members of the public as well as legislators had urged that "the observance of distinctive urban and rural communities of interest should be a prime consideration in the general redistricting process. As a result, the legislature was naturally attracted to a plan that, although less than aesthetically pleasing, included both District 12, which links the State's major urban centers, and District 1, which has a population that predominantly lives in cities with populations of less than 20,000.

Moreover, the record reveals that District 12's lines were drawn in order to unite an African-American community whose political tradition was quite distinct from the one that defines African-American voters in the Coastal Plain, which District 1 surrounds. Ibid. Indeed, two other majority-minority-district plans with less torturous boundaries were thought unsatisfactory precisely because they did not unite communities of interest. . . .

III

As the foregoing discussion illustrates, legislative decisions are often the product of compromise and mixed motives. For that reason, I have always been skeptical about the value of motivational analysis as a basis for constitutional adjudication. I am particularly skeptical of such an inquiry in a case of this type, as mixed motivations would seem to be endemic to the endeavor of political districting.

The majority's analysis of the "compelling interest" issue nicely demonstrates the problem with parsing legislative motive in this context. The majority posits that the legislature's compelling interest in drawing District 12 was its desire to avoid liability under §2 of the Voting Rights Act. Yet it addresses the question whether North Carolina had a compelling interest only because it first concludes that a racial purpose dominated the State's districting effort.

It seems to me that if the State's true purpose were to serve its compelling interest in staving off costly litigation by complying with federal law, then it cannot be correct to say that a racially discriminatory purpose controlled its line-drawing. A more accurate conclusion would be that the State took race into account only to the extent necessary to meet the requirements of a carefully thought out federal statute. The majority's implicit equation of the intentional consideration of race in order to comply with the Voting Rights Act with intentional racial discrimination reveals the inadequacy of the framework it adopts for considering the constitutionality of race-based districting.

However, even if I were to assume that strict scrutiny applies, and thus that it makes sense to consider the question, I would not share the majority's hesitancy in concluding that North Carolina had a "compelling interest" in drawing District 12. . . .

First, some legislators felt that the sorry history of race relations in North Carolina in past decades was a sufficient reason for making it easier for more black leaders to participate in the legislative process and to represent the State in the Congress of the United States. Even if that history does not provide the kind of precise guidance that will justify certain specific affirmative action programs in particular industries, it surely provides an adequate basis for a decision to facilitate the election of representatives of the previously disadvantaged minority. . . .

Second, regardless of whether §5 of the Act was actually violated, I believe the State's interest in avoiding the litigation that would have been necessary to overcome the Attorney General's objection to the original plan provides an acceptable reason for creating a second majority-minority district. . . .

IV . . .

In my judgment, if a State's new plan successfully avoids the potential litigation entirely, there is no reason why it must also take the form of a "remedy" for an unproven violation. Thus, the fact that no §2 violation has been proven in the territory that comprises District 12 does not show that the district fails to serve a compelling state interest. It shows only that a federal court, which is constrained by Article III, would not have had the power to require North Carolina to draw that district. It is axiomatic that a State should have more authority to institute a districting plan than would a federal court. . . .

V . . .

Because I have no hesitation in concluding that North Carolina's decision to adopt a plan in which white voters were in the majority in only 10 of the State's 12 districts did not violate the Equal Protection Clause, I respectfully dissent.

JUSTICE SOUTER, with whom JUSTICE GINSBURG and JUSTICE BREYER join, dissenting.

My views on this case are substantially expressed in my dissent to Bush v. Vera.

Page 1016. At the end of section 3 of the Note, add the following:

See Frances Myrna Kamm, Abortion and Creation 98 (1992):

> (1) It may be wrong if it suggests that abortion would be morally impermissible if its permissibility were not necessary to achieve social equality (that is, if women were socially dominant to men, [would] abortion be impermissible?). (2) It may be wrong if it claims that one may kill someone simply because this is necessary for social equality. [One] cannot kill infants [if] their existence led to social inequality for women because women but not men could not resist taking care of them.

Page 1016. At the end of section 5 of the Note, add the following:

For general discussion of what burdens should be deemed incidental, and of why and when it matters, see Dorf, Incidental Burdens on Fundamental Rights, 109 Harv. L. Rev. 1175 (1996).

Page 1045. After the first full paragraph on the page, ending with "the particular medical treatment is specified", add:

JUSTICE STEVENS, dissenting.

Page 1048. Before "G. Procedural Due Process," add the following:

Note: Punitive Damages and Substantive Due Process

Can an award of punitive damages be so excessive as to violate the due process clause in its substantive dimension? A majority of the Court concluded that it can in BMW of North America v. Gore, 116 S. Ct. 1589 (1996). Dr. Gore had sought punitive damages because his new BMW had actually been repainted, and he was not informed of this fact. The jury granted an award of punitive damages that was very large in comparison to the compensatory damages awarded in the case. There was a $4000 compensatory award and a $4 million punitive award.

Presented by this disparity, the Court ruled for the first time that an award of punitive damages violates the due process clause. (In a set of past cases the Court had left the issue open.) But there was an important internal division. The opinion for the Court spoke in terms of a form of substantive due process. Justice Breyer's concurring opinion did not reject this characterization, but it was procedurally oriented.

In finding the award grossly excessive, the Court referred to three points: the degree of reprehensibility, the ratio of punitive to compensatory damages, and the available penalties for comparable misconduct.

First, the Court said that nothing was especially horrible about BMW's behavior. There was no effect on performance or safety of the car, no indifference to or reckless disregard for health and safety. The failure to disclose the relevant material was very plausibly a wrong, but not a matter of egregious affirmative misconduct. (Thus the judgment about reprehensibility seemed to focus on both harm and state of mind.) Second, the ratio of punitive damages to compensatory damages was especially bad.

Third, the civil and criminal penalties that could be imposed for comparable misconduct were far more limited, involving, for example, a maximum civil penalty for deceptive trade practices of $2000. The Court also emphasized the state's lack of power to enact policies for the entire nation, or to impose its own policies on other states. Economic penalties must therefore be supported by the state's interest in protecting its own consumers and economy, rather than those of other states. The award therefore had to be analyzed in light of conduct within Alabama, and could not include conduct elsewhere.

Justice Breyer pressed some different points. He suggested that the most serious problem was not sheer excessiveness but the absence of legal standards that could reduce decisionmaker caprice. Here the relevant standards "are vague and open-ended to the point where they risk arbitrary results." The jury operated under no statute with standards distinguishing among permissible punitive damage awards. In Alabama, the seven factors used to constrain punitive damages awards have not been applied in a way that makes up for actual constraint. Nor have the state courts made any effort to discipline those factors in such a way as to generate a legally constraining standard. The excessiveness of the penalty combined with the absence of procedural safeguards to justify a judgment that the due process clause had been violated.

Justice Scalia wrote a dissenting opinion, joined by Justice Thomas, suggesting that this was a form of substantive due process that was entirely illegitimate. In Justice Scalia's view, punitive damage judgments should be left to the states. Justice Ginsburg also dissented, in an opinion joined by Justice Rehnquist, suggesting that states were actively considering the issue and coming close to the Scalia-Thomas position.

After *BMW,* it is clear that a majority of the Court is willing to hold that an award of punitive damages may be excessive and therefore inconsistent with substantive due process. How does this line of analysis compare with other cases in which the Court has used substantive due process to invalidate legislation? Is it more or less legitimate?

See also Bennis v. Michigan, 116 S. Ct. 1560 (1996). There the Court upheld, against procedural due process challenge, a forfeiture scheme operating against an admittedly innocent property owner. Bennis was a joint owner, with her husband, of a car that had been forfeited as a public nuisance because her husband was found engaged in the automobile in illegal sexual activity with a prostitute. Bennis lacked knowledge of the activity and claimed that it was unconstitutional not to allow an "innocent owner" defense. The Court concluded that past cases had said the Constitution did not recognize the defense and that in any case the absence of such a defense prevented evasion by dispensing with the need for a judicial inquiry into possible collusion. Justice Stevens dissented, in an opinion joined by Justices Souter and Breyer.

Chapter Seven

Freedom of Expression

A. INTRODUCTION

Page 1080. Before section 2 of the Note, add the following:

e. Marshall, In Defense of the Search for Truth as a First Amendment Justification, 30 Ga. L. Rev. 1, 2-5 (1995):

> In the contemporary postmodern world, the notion that there is positive value in the search for truth would strike some as a quaint anachronism. [To] the contemporary mind, objective or transcendent truth is seen as nonsensical. . . . The Enlightenment claim that the powers of reason could lead humanity to a knowledge of truth has been savaged. [Although] objective truth may [be] nonexistent, [this] attack misfires when it suggests that the First Amendment value inherent in the search for truth exists only in [the] actual finding of truth. The value that is to be realized is not in the possible attainment of truth, but rather, in the existential value of the search itself.

But "can there be First Amendment value in pursuing what is considered likely to be unattainable [and] unintelligible?" Marshall, supra, at 8.

B. CONTENT-BASED RESTRICTIONS: DANGEROUS IDEAS AND INFORMATION

Page 1086. Before section 5 of the Note, add the following:

d. *Speech as a property right.* For the view that "the function of the First Amendment is not to promote the collective interest in self-governance, [but] to prohibit regulation of an important property right peculiarly threatened by the government," see McGinnis, The Once and Future Property-Based Vision of the First Amendment, 63 U. Chi. L. Rev. 49, 57 (1996).

Page 1139. At the end of the first paragraph on the page, after the cite to Stone, add the following:

Kagan, Private Speech, Public Purpose: The Role of Governmental Motive in First Amendment Doctrine, 63 U. Chi. L. Rev. 415, 431-432 (1996) ("the government may not limit speech because other citizens deem the ideas offered to be wrong or offensive [because] the First Amendment protects no less against majority oppression than against runaway government").

C. OVERBREADTH, VAGUENESS, AND PRIOR RESTRAINT

Page 1185. At the end of the third line, add the following:

See Kagan, Private Speech, Public Purpose: The Role of Governmental Motive in First Amendment Doctrine, 63 U. Chi. L. Rev. 415, 459-463 (1996) ("the rule against standardless licensing [serves the] function of flushing out bad motive by establishing a safeguard against administrative action based on the content of expression").

D. CONTENT-BASED RESTRICTIONS: "LOW" VALUE SPEECH

Page 1244. Before the Note, add the following:

44 LIQUORMART, INC. v. RHODE ISLAND, 116 S. CT. 1495 (1996): In a divided set of opinions, the Court invalidated a Rhode Island statute prohibiting "advertising in any manner whatsoever" of the price of any alcoholic beverage offered for sale in the State, except for price tags or signs displayed within licensed premises and not visible from the street.

Justice Stevens delivered a plurality opinion joined by Justices Kennedy and Ginsburg, and joined in different parts by Justices Souter and Thomas: "As [a] review of our case law reveals, [not] all commercial speech regulations are subject to a similar form of constitutional [review]. When a State regulates commercial messages to protect consumers from misleading, deceptive, or aggressive sales practices, or requires the disclosure of beneficial consumer information, the purpose of its regulation is consistent with the reasons for according constitutional protection to commercial speech and therefore justifies less than strict review.

"However, when a State entirely prohibits the dissemination of truthful, nonmisleading commercial messages for reasons unrelated to the preservation of a fair bargaining process, there is far less reason to depart from the rigorous review that the First Amendment generally demands. [Citing

Linmark; *Virginia Pharmacy*; and *Went For It.*] The special dangers that attend complete bans on truthful, nonmisleading commercial speech cannot be explained away by appeals to the 'commonsense distinctions' that exist between commercial and noncommercial speech. [Neither] the 'greater objectivity' nor the 'greater hardiness' of truthful, nonmisleading commercial speech justifies reviewing its complete suppression with added deference. [Bans] against truthful, nonmisleadng commercial speech [usually] rest solely on the offensive assumption that the public will respond 'irrationally' to the truth. The First Amendment directs us to be especially skeptical of regulations that seek to keep people in the dark for what the government perceives to be their own good. That teaching applies equally to state attempts to deprive consumers of accurate information about their chosen products. . . .

"The State argues that the price advertising prohibition should [be] upheld because it directly advances the State's substantial interest in promoting tolerance, and because it is no more extensive than necessary. [We] can agree that common sense supports the conclusion that a prohibition against price advertising [will] tend to [maintain] prices at a higher level than would prevail in a completely free market [and that] consumption [is likely to be] somewhat lower whenever a higher, noncompetitive price level prevails. However, without any [evidentiary] support [we] cannot agree with the assertion that the price advertising ban will significantly advance the State's interest. . . . [Speculation about such matters] does not suffice when the State takes aim at accurate commercial information for paternalistic ends. . . .

"The State also cannot satisfy the requirement that its restriction on speech be no more extensive than necessary. It is perfectly obvious that alternative forms of regulation that would not involve any restriction on speech would be more likely to achieve the State's goal of promoting temperance. [Higher] prices can be maintained either by direct regulation or by increased taxation. Per capita purchases could be limited as is the case with prescription drugs. Even educational campaigns focused on the problems [of] drinking might prove to be more effective. As a result, even under the less than strict standard that generally applies in commercial speech cases, the State has failed to establish a 'reasonable fit' between its abridgment of speech and its temperance goal. [It] necessarily follows that the price advertising ban cannot survive the more stringent constitutional review that *Central Hudson* itself concluded was appropriate for the complete suppression of truthful, nonmisleading commercial speech. . . .

"Relying on *Posadas* and *Edge Broadcasting*, Rhode Island [argues] that, because expert opinions as to the effectiveness of the price advertising ban 'go both ways' [the legislation should be upheld as] a 'reasonable choice' by the legislature. The State next contends that *Posadas* requires us to give particular deference to that legislative choice because the State could, if it chose, ban the sale of alcoholic beverages outright. Finally, the State argues that deference is appropriate because alcoholic beverages are so-called 'vice' products. We consider each of these arguments in turn.

"The State's first argument fails [because the State] errs in concluding that *Edge* and *Posadas* establish the degree of deference that [is appropriate in this case.] In *Edge*, [the] statute [regulated] advertising about an activity that [was] illegal in the jurisdiction in which the broadcaster was located. Here, by contrast, the commercial speech ban targets information about entirely lawful behavior. *Posadas* is more directly relevant. [But] we are now persuaded that [*Posadas*] clearly erred in concluding that it was 'up to the legislature' to choose suppression over a less speech-restrictive policy. [In] keeping with [our pre-*Posadas*] holdings, we conclude that a state legislature does not [have] broad discretion to suppress truthful, nonmisleading information for paternalistic purposes. . . .

"We also cannot accept the State's second contention, which is premised [on] the 'greater-includes-the-lesser' reasoning endorsed [in] *Posadas*. [This reasoning] is inconsistent with both logic and well-settled doctrine. [Contrary] to the assumption made in *Posadas*, [the] Constitution presumes that attempts to regulate speech are more dangerous than attempts to regulate conduct. [As] the entire Court apparently now agrees, the statements in [*Posadas*] on which Rhode Island relies are no longer persuasive.

"Finally, we [reject] the State's contention that [the] price advertising ban should be upheld because it targets commercial speech that pertains to a 'vice' activity. [The] scope of any 'vice' exception to the protection afforded by the First Amendment would be difficult, if not impossible, to define. . . .

"Because Rhode Island has failed to carry its heavy burden of justifying its complete ban on price advertising, we conclude that [the challenged legislation is unconstitutional]."

Justice Scalia concurred in the judgment. Scalia observed that, "where the core offense of suppressing particular political ideas is not at issue," the Court should interpret the first amendment in light of "the long accepted practices of the American people," with particular reference to "the state legislative practices prevalent at the time" the first and fourteenth amendments were adopted. Because the parties in this case provided "no evidence on these points," however, Scalia concluded that the legislation was invalid under the Court's "existing jurisprudence."

Justice Thomas also filed a concurring opinion: "In cases such as this, in which the government's asserted interest is to keep legal users of a product or service ignorant in order to manipulate their choices in the marketplace, the balancing test adopted in *Central Hudson* should not be applied. [Such] an 'interest' is per se illegitimate and can no more justify regulation of 'commercial' speech than it can justify regulation of 'noncommercial' speech. [Both] Justice Stevens and Justice O'Connor appear to adopt a stricter [interpretation] of *Central Hudson* than that suggested in some of our other opinions, one that could [go] a long way toward the position I take. [But] rather than 'applying' [*Central Hudson*] to reach the inevitable result [in this case], I would [hold that] all attempts to dissuade legal choices by citizens by keeping them ignorant are impermissible."

Justice O'Connor, joined by Chief Justice Rehnquist and Justices Souter and Breyer, all filed an opinion concurring in the judgment: "[This legislation] fails the final prong [of *Central Hudson*]; that is, its ban is more extensive than necessary to serve the State's interest. [The] fit between Rhode Island's method and [its] goal is not reasonable. [As demonstrated by Justice Stevens, the] State has other methods at its disposal—methods that would more directly accomplish [its] goal without intruding on sellers' ability to provide truthful, nonmisleading information to customers. [The State points] for support to *Posadas*. Since *Posadas*, however, this Court has examined more searchingly the State's professed goal, and the speech restriction put into place to further it, before accepting a State's claim that the speech restriction satisfies First Amendment scrutiny. [Citing, e.g., *Went for It* and *Coors Brewing*]. [Because the challenged legislation] fails even [the] standard set out in *Central Hudson*, nothing here requires the adoption of a new analysis for the evaluation of commercial speech regulation."

Page 1252. Before section 2 of the Note, add the following:

Consider also Hamilton, Art Speech, 49 Vand. L. Rev. 73, 77-78 (1996):

> [A]rt cannot receive its due as long as attempts to justify its place in the pantheon of first amendment freedoms are focused only upon the protection of ideas or information. Art can carry ideas and information, but it also goes beyond logical, rational, and discursive communication. [A] strong analogy can be drawn between the protection of art and the protection of religion. . . . Art and religion form a prism through which the First Amendment is transformed from a haven for ideas to a means of protecting vital spheres of personal freedom. [Art] construct[s] paths out of repression [and helps to preserve] the constitutional balance between the governed and the governing. [Art serves an] integral function in a successful representative democracy, [for it] provides the opportunity to experience alternative worlds and therefore to gain distance and perspective on the prevailing status quo.

Page 1297. At the end of section 3 of the Note, add the following:

In 44 Liquormart, Inc. v. Rhode Island, 116 S. Ct. 1495 (1996), the Court disavowed *LaRue's* reliance on the twenty-first amendment, concluding that the twenty-first amendment does not qualify the first amendment's prohibition against laws abridging the freedom of speech.

Page 1297. At the end of the first paragraph of section 5 of the Note, add the following:

See also American Civil Liberties Union v. Reno, 1996 U.S. Dist. LEXIS 7919 (E.D. Pa. 1996) (invalidating as unconstitutionally vague and overbroad the 1996 Communications Decency Act, which prohibited any person from sending over the Internet in a way that would be available to a person under 18 years of age any "indecent material," which was defined in the Act as any material that "in context, depicts or describes, in terms patently offensive as measured by contemporary community standards, sexual or excretory activities or organs").

Page 1298. Before Section 6, add the following:

DENVER AREA EDUCATIONAL TELECOMMUNICATIONS CONSORTIUM, INC. v. FCC, 116 S. CT. — (1996): In the Cable Act of 1984, Congress required cable operators to reserve approximately 15 percent of their channels for commercial lease to "unaffiliated persons." In addition, the Act authorized local governments to require cable operators to set aside a certain number of channels for "public, educational, or governmental use." The 1984 Act expressly prohibited cable operators from exercising any editorial control over the content of programs broadcast on either "leased access" or "public access" channels. In this case, the Court considered the constitutionality of three provisions of the Cable Television Consumer Protection and Competition Act of 1992, which altered this scheme with respect "indecent progamming," defined as programming that depicts or describes "sexual activities or organs in a patently offensive manner."

Section 10(a). This provision authorized cable operators to prohibit programming they "believe to be indecent," as defined above, on leased access channels. In defense of this provision, the FCC argued that a cable operator is analogous to a newspaper, which, as a private actor, can refuse to carry such material without violating the first amendment. The FCC maintained that section 10(a) does nothing more than to give a cable operator, also a private actor, the same authority as a newspaper. Petitioners (a consortium of leased access channel "unaffiliated" programmers) offered a different view of the matter. Noting that section 10(a) is an exception to the general prohibition against cable operators exercising editorial control over leased-access programming, petitioners argued that section 10(a) is an unconstitutional content-based restriction because it authorizes cable operators to exercise editorial control over only this form of expression. In a seven-to-two decision, the Court upheld this provision.

In a plurality opinion, Justice Breyer, joined by Justices Stevens, O'Connor, and Souter, concluded that section 10(a) does not violate the first amendment. Noting "the changes taking place in the law, the technology, and the industrial structure related to telecommunications," Breyer maintained that the Court should "decide this case . . . narrowly, by closely scrutinizing §10(a) to assure that it properly addresses an extremely important problem, without imposing [an] unnecessarily great restriction on speech."

Applying that approach, Breyer invoked several considerations to justify his conclusion. First, "the provision [serves] an extremely important justification—the need to protect children from exposure to patently offensive sex-related material." Second, "the provision arises in a very particular context—congressional permission to regulate programming that, but for a previous Act of Congress, would have [no access to such channels] free of an operator's control." Third, "the problem Congress addressed here is remarkably similar to the problem addressed [in] *Pacifica*." Fourth, "the permissive nature of §10(a) means that it likely restricts speech less than, not more than, the ban at issue in *Pacifica*," for cable operators need not exercise the authority granted them under the Act. In light of these considerations, Breyer concluded that "the permissive nature of the provision, coupled with its viewpoint-neutral application, [suggests that section 10(a) is] a constitutionally permissible way to protect [children], while accommodating both the First Amendment interests served by the access requirements and those served in restoring to cable operators a degree of the editorial control that Congress removed in 1984."

Justice Thomas, joined by Chief Justice Rehnquist and Justice Scalia, concurred in the result. Thomas took a very different approach, however. In Thomas's view, programmers have no first amendment "right to transmit over an operator's cable system." Thomas drew an "analogy to the print media" where, "for example, the author of a book [has] no right to have the book sold in a particular bookstore without the store owner's consent." Thus, "the proper question" posed by these regulations is not whether section 10(a) violates the "free speech rights" of programmers, but whether "the leased and public access requirements [are] improper restrictions on the operators' free speech rights." Returning to the print media analogy, Thomas observed that if "Congress passed a law forcing bookstores to sell books published on the subject of congressional politics, we would undoubtedly entertain a claim by bookstores that this law violated the First Amendment, [but] I doubt we would similarly find merit in a claim by publishers of gardening books that the law violated their First Amendment rights." Thomas concluded that, "if that is so, then the petitioners [cannot] reasonably assert that the Court should strictly scrutinize [section 10(a)] in a way that maximizes their ability to speak [and], by necessity, minimizes the operators' discretion."

Justice Kennedy, joined by Justice Ginsburg, dissented. At the outset, Kennedy sharply criticized the plurality for applying "no standard" and for losing "sight of existing First Amendment doctrine." Kennedy argued that, "when confronted with a threat to free speech in the context of an emerging technology, we ought to have the discipline to analyze the case by reference to existing elaborations of constant First Amendment principles," not "wander into uncharted areas of the law with no compass other than our own opinions about good policy." In Kennedy's view, the issue here is "straightforward" and provides "no reason to discard our existing First Amendment jurisprudence."

Kennedy emphasized that in section 10(a), "Congress singles out one sort of speech for vulnerability to private censorship in a context where [it does not otherwise permit] content-based discrimination." Specifically, section 10(a) expressly disadvantages "nonobscene, indecent programming, a protected category of expression, [citing *Sable*], on the basis of its content." In such circumstances, Kennedy observed, "strict scrutiny applies," and however "compelling Congress' interest in shielding children from indecent programming," section 10(a) "cannot survive this exacting review." This is so, Kennedy argued, because "to the extent cable operators prohibit indecent programming on access channels, not only children but adults will be deprived of it," and in light of the availability of other means of regulating such expression, such as blocking mechanisms available to individual subscribers, the government "has no legitimate interest in making access channels pristine."

Finally, Kennedy rejected the government's argument that, under *Pacifica*, a lower standard of review is appropriate for regulations of "indecent" speech. Echoing *Cohen*, Kennedy maintained that, in "artistic or political settings, indecency may have strong communicative content, protesting conventional norms or giving an edge to a work by conveying 'otherwise inexpressible emotions.'" Moreover, indecent speech "often is inseparable from the ideas and viewpoints conveyed, or separable only with the loss of truth or expressive power." Thus, such restrictions should be permitted only if they are "narrowly tailored to serve a compelling interest."

Section 10(c). This section is essentially identical to section 10(a), but regulates public access rather than leased-access channels. In a 5-4 decision, the Court invalidated section 10(c). In a plurality opinion, Justice Breyer, joined by Justices Stevens and Souter, identified "four important differences" that, in their view, distinguished section 10(c) from section 10(a). First, "cable operators have traditionally agreed to reserve channel capacity for public [access] channels as part of the consideration they give municipalities that award them cable franchises. [Thus], these are channels over which cable operators have not historically exercised editorial control. Unlike §10(a) therefore, §10(c) does not restore to cable operators editorial rights that they once had." Second, unlike leased access channels, where "the lessee has total control of programming during the leased time slot," public-access channels "are normally subject to complex supervisory systems [with] public and private elements." Third, because in the public-access context there is already in place "a locally accountable body capable of addressing the problem [of] patently offensive programming broadcast to children," there is less need for a "cable operator's veto" to "achieve the statute's objective." Fourth, there is no "factual basis" demonstrating that the existing mechanisms of control for public-access channels are not sufficient to address the statute's concern. "The upshot," Breyer concluded, is that "the Government cannot sustain its burden of showing that §10(c) is necessary to protect children or that it is appropriately tailored to secure that end."

Justice Kennedy, joined by Justice Ginsburg, concurred in the result. Although rejecting Justice Breyer's reasoning, Kennedy concluded that section 10(c) is unconstitutional for essentially the same reasons he thought section 10(a) is unconstitutional.

Justice O'Connor dissented because she was not "persuaded" that "the asserted 'important differences'" that Justice Breyer identified to distinguish section 10(a) from section 10(c) "are sufficient to justify striking down §10(c)." In her view, both provisions are constitutional.

Justice Thomas, joined by Chief Justice Rehnquist and Justice Scalia, dissented. In their view, section 10(c) is constitutional for the same reasons he thought section 10(a) is constitutional.

Section 10(b). This section of the Act, which applies only to leased-access channels, requires cable operators to segregate "indecent" programming on a single channel, to block that channel from viewer access, and to unblock it only on a subscriber's written request (and within thirty days of receiving the request). The Court, in a 6-3 decision, invalidated this provision. Justice Breyer delivered the opinion of the Court. At the outset, the Court noted that this provision "significantly differs" from sections 10(a) and 10(c) because "it does not simply permit, but rather requires cable operators to restrict [such] speech." The Court observed that this provision has "obvious restrictive effects" on the access of individuals to this sort of programming, including the potential chilling effect of the "written notice" requirement on subscribers who may "fear for their reputations should the operator, advertently or inadvertently, disclose the list of those who wish to watch the 'patently offensive' channel."

The Court found it unnecessary to "determine whether, or the extent to which, *Pacifica* does, or does not, impose some lesser standard of review where indecent speech is at issue." Although agreeing with the government that the "protection of children is a 'compelling interest,'" the Court concluded that the provision is nonetheless invalid because "it is not a 'least restrictive alternative,'" is "not 'narrowly tailored,'" and is "'more extensive than necessary.'" Thus, "it fails to satisfy this Court's formulations of the First Amendment's 'strictest,' as well as its somewhat less 'strict,' requirements." The most important consideration leading the Court to this conclusion was the availability of other, less speech-restrictive, means to achieve the objective of the provision. Other legislation, for example, governing channels other than leased-access channels, "requires cable operators to [scramble] such programming"; requires cable operators to "honor a subscriber's request to block any, or all, programs on any channel to which he or she does not wish to subscribe"; requires cable operators to provide subscribers, on request, with a "lockbox," which enables parents "to 'lock out' those programs or channels that they [do] not want their children to see"; and requires "manufacturers, in the future, [to] make television sets with a so-called 'V-chip'—a device that will be able automatically to identify and block sexually explicit or violent programs." Although not deciding "whether these [alternative] provisions are themselves unlawful," the Court emphasized that "they are significantly less restrictive than the provision here at issue." Although "conceding" that "no provision, [short] of an absolute ban, can offer certain protection against assault by a determined child," the Court emphasized that it has not "generally allowed this fact alone to justify 'reduc[ing] the adult population [to] only what is fit for children.'"

Justice Thomas, joined by Chief Justice Rehnquist and Justice Scalia, dissented. Although conceding that "§10(b) must be subjected to strict scrutiny and can be upheld only if it furthers a compelling governmental interest by the least restrictive means available," Thomas concluded that section 10(b) satisfies this standard. After asserting that "Congress has 'a compelling [interest in] shielding minors from the influence of [indecent speech] that is not obscene by adult standards," Thomas turned to his disagreement with the Court: "The Court strikes down §10(b) by pointing to alternatives, such as reverse-blocking and lockboxes, that it says are less restrictive than segregation and blocking. Though these methods attempt to place in parents' hands the ability to permit their children to watch as little, or as much, indecent programming as the parents think proper, they do not effectively support parents' authority to direct the moral upbringing of their children. [Because] indecent programming on leased access channels is 'especially likely to be shown randomly or intermittently between non-indecent programs, [parents] armed with only a lockbox must carefully monitor all leased-access programming and constantly reprogram the lockbox to keep out undesired programming. [This] characteristic of leased access channels makes lockboxes and reverse-blocking largely ineffective."

Thomas also dismissed the Court's concern that section 10(b) requires subscribers who want access to indecent programming to give written consent. Thomas argued that if a segregation and blocking scheme is otherwise permissible, then it can hardly be invalidated because subscribers must request access, for any "request for access to blocked programming—by whatever method—ultimately will make the subscriber's identity knowable. But this is hardly the kind of chilling effect that implicates the First Amendment."

E. CONTENT-NEUTRAL RESTRICTIONS: MEANS OF COMMUNICATION

Page 1330. At the end of section 1 of the Note, add the following:

Kagan, Private Speech, Public Purpose: The Role of Governmental Motive in First Amendment Doctrine, 63 U. Chi. L. Rev. 415, 446-463 (1996) (arguing that the concern with improper government motivatation best explains the content-based/content-neutral distinction).

Page 1375. Before section 5 of the Note, add the following:

4a. *Cable television: public access channels.* In the Cable Act of 1984, Congress authorized local governments to require cable operators to set aside a certain number of channels for "public, educational, or governmental use." The 1984 Act expressly prohibited cable operators from exercising any editorial control over the content of programs broadcast on "public access" channels. In the Cable Television Consumer Protection and Competition Act of 1992, Congress amended this scheme to authorize cable operators to restrict "indecent" programming on public access channels. "Indecent" programming is defined as programming that the cable operator "reasonably believes depicts or describes sexual activities or organs in a patently offensive manner." In Denver Area Education Telecommunications Consortium, Inc. v. FCC, supra section VII-D-5, this Supplement, the Court invalidated this provision. Although the Court as a whole did not decide whether a public-access channel constitutes a "designated public forum," several of the Justices did debate the issue. Consider the following views:

a. Justice Kennedy, joined by Justice Ginsburg:

> [P]ublic access channels [are] available at low or no cost to members of the public, often on a first-come, first-served basis. [They clearly] meet the definition of a [designated] public forum. [The] House Report for the 1984 Cable Act is consistent with this view. It characterizes public access channels as "the video equivalent of the speaker's soapbox or [the] printed leaflet." [We] need not decide here any broad issue of whether private property can be declared a public

forum by simple governmental decree. That is not what happens in the creation of public access channels. Rather, in return for granting cable operators easements to use public rights-of-way for their cable lines, local governments have bargained for a right to use cable lines for public access channels. [It] seems to me clear that when a local government contracts to use private property for public expressive activity [in this manner], it creates a public forum.

b. Justice Stevens:

In my view, [Congress has not] established a public forum. [When] the federal government opens cable channels that would otherwise be left in private hands, it deserves more deference than a rigid application of the public forum doctrine would allow. At this early stage in the regulation of this developing industry, Congress should not be put to an all or nothing-at-all choice in deciding whether to open certain cable channels to programmers who would otherwise lack the resources to participate in the marketplace of ideas. [If] the Government had a reasonable basis for concluding that there were already enough classical musical programs or cartoons being telecast—or, perhaps, even enough political debate—I would find no First Amendment objection to an open access requirement that was extended on an impartial basis to all but those particular subjects. A contrary conclusion would ill-serve First Amendment values by dissuading the Government from creating access rights altogether.

c. Justice Thomas, joined by Chief Justice Rehnquist and Justice Scalia:

[P]ublic access channels are [not] public fora. [Cable] systems are not public property. Cable systems are privately owned and privately managed, and [there is] no case is which we have held that government may designate private property as a public forum. [It] may be true [that] title is not dispositive of the public forum analysis, but the nature of the regulatory restrictions placed on cable operators by local franchising authorities are not consistent with the kinds of governmental property interests we have said may be formally dedicated as public fora. Our public forum cases have involved property in which the government has held at least some formal easement or other property interest permitting the government to treat the property as its own in designating the property as a public forum. That is simply not true [here]. [Public] access requirements [are merely] a regulatory restriction on the exercise of cable operators' editorial discretion, not a transfer of a sufficient property interest in the channels to support a designation of that property as a public forum.

Page 1385. At the end of section 1 of the Note, add the following:

Consider the argument that *Rust* can be understood as a misapplication of the principle underlying *Posadas* : "Under the *Posadas* rationale, viewpoint-based suppression of speech simply was not an issue because the Court viewed casino advertising as an activity and not as speech. [The] *Rust*

Court's reasoning was similar; because abortion counseling was merely an activity within the Title X project, it was not subject to traditional strictures of the First Amendment. Thus, as casino gambling was to gambling, abortion counseling was to abortion." Wells, Abortion Counseling as Vice Activity: The Free Speech Implications of *Rust v. Sullivan* and *Planned Parenthood v. Casey*, 95 Colum. L. Rev. 1724, 1749 (1995).

Page 1385. At the end of section 2 of the Note, add the following:

Consider also Redish and Kessler, Government Subsidies and Free Expression, 80 Minn. L. Rev. 543, 576-577 (1996):

> The problem with the [Court's analysis in *Rust*] is that it allows the government to define its subsidization programs in a wholly unchecked, self-referential manner. [The] fallacy of [this approach] becomes clear if one visualizes the subsidization of private expression exclusively in favor of such ideas as a free-market economic philosophy, or the political theories of Mao Zedong or Rush Limbaugh. [Government] may appropriately choose neutrally to fund works on family planning, on the viability of free-market economic philosophy, or on the wisdom of Mao Zedong's or Rush Limbaugh's political thought. Each of these subsidies would foster First Amendment values by adding to the public's knowledge. [But] government may not foster public acceptance of its own viewpoints on these issues by manipulating private expression [in a viewpoint-based manner].

Page 1395. At the end of section 6 of the Note, add the following:

Kagan, Private Speech, Public Purpose: The Role of Governmental Motive in First Amendment Doctrine, 63 U. Chi. L. Rev. 415, 494-508 (1996) (arguing that the distinction between direct and incidential restrictions in first amendment analysis can be explained largely in terms of the concern with avoiding possible improper governmental motivation).

Page 1404. At the end of *Barnes*, add the following:

For the argument that "the outcome in *Barnes* would have been different" had Indiana attempted to apply its "statute to accepted media for the communication of ideas, as for example by attempting to prohibit nudity in movies or in the theater," see Post, Recuperating First Amendment Doctrine, 47 Stan. L. Rev. 1249, 1255-1259 (1995) (arguing that "[c]rucial to the result in *Barnes* [is] the distinction between what the Court is prepared to accept as a medium for the communication of ideas and its implicit understanding of nude dancing in nightclubs").

Page 1419. After the quotation from BeVier, add the following:

Consider Kagan, Private Speech, Public Purpose: The Role of Governmental Motive in First Amendment Doctrine, 63 U. Chi. L. Rev. 415, 467-475 (1996):

> In what has become one of the most castigated passages in modern First Amendment case law, the Court pronounced in *Buckley v. Valeo* that "the concept that government may restrict the speech of some elements of our society in order to enhance the relative voice of others is wholly foreign to the First Amendment. . . ." [The] *Buckley* principle emerges not from the view that redistribution of speech opportunities is itself an illegitimate end, but from the view that governmental actions justified as redistributive devices often (though not always) stem partly from hostility or sympathy toward ideas—or, even more commonly, from self-interest. [The] nature of [such] regulations, as compared with other content-neutral regulations, creates [a special problem]: that governmental officials (here, legislators) more often will take account of improper factors. [This] increased probability of taint arises [from] the very design of laws directed at equalizing the realm of public expression. Unlike most content-neutral regulations, these laws not only have, but are supposed to have, content-based effects. . . . In considering such a law, a legislator's own views of the ideas (or speakers) that the equalization effort means to suppress or promote may well intrude, consciously or not, on her decision making process. [Thus,] there may be good reason to distrust the motives of politicians when they apply themselves to reconstructing the realm of expression.

Page 1425. Before section 1 of the Note, add the following:

1a. *Corporate speakers.* To what extent, if any, should corporations enjoy the freedom of speech? In Pacific Gas & Electric Co. v. Public Utilities Commission of California, section F3, infra, page 1468 of the main volume, Chief Justice Rehnquist observed in a separate opinion that "[e]xtension of [first amendment protection to corporations based on] individual freedom of conscience [strains] the rationale [of the first amendment beyond] the breaking point. To ascribe to such artificial entities an 'intellect' or 'mind' [is] to confuse metaphor with reality." Consider also Bezanson, Institutional Speech, 80 Iowa L. Rev. 735, 755, 761, 739 (1995):

> [S]peech is fundamentally a human act, [and] for purposes of the First Amendment, protected speech is primarily a product of the human act of speaking. [Under] the First Amendment, meaning and intention, speech and authorship, are inextricably tied together, and therefore it is critically important that protected speech originate in a human agent acting in a willful communicative way to express his or her ideas. . . .
>
> [T]he First Amendment contains within it two theoretical elements: one concerning individual liberty and freedom of thought, and the other concerning the value of free information and opinion in a democratic and free society.

> [The] First Amendment should be understood as principally [a] protection for individual speech, or speech that reflects an individual's liberty to engage in the voluntary and intentional act of expressing his or her own beliefs. [Institutional] speech, in contrast, is abstracted from the individual. [It] has nothing to do with liberty and no necessary relationship to freedom, a term that is meaningless outside the context of individuals. [Institutional speech] can lay no legitimate claim to protection under the heading of individual liberty, and thus must be assessed only in terms of the second element relating to the functional value of speech in a democratic and free society. [Institutional] speech, therefore, should be protected by a separate and distinct framework [and] should be judged not by standards of freedom, but by broader and more forgiving criteria that relate to the information needed by the members of a free and self-governing society. Such criteria would permit not only an assessment of institutional speech's value, but also its manner of presentation (accuracy, for example) and the medium of its distribution (fairness, access, and market conditions).

Page 1425. Before section 2 of the Note, add the following:

1a. *Regulating political parties.* After *Buckley*, can the government constitutionally limit the amount a political party can spend in support of its own candidates? Are such expenditures "contributions" or "expenditures" within the meaning of *Buckley*? In Colorado Republican Federal Campaign Committee v. Federal Election Commission, 116 S. Ct. — (1996), the Court considered the constitutionality of a provision of the Federal Election Campaign Act that imposes dollar limits on political party "expenditures in connection with the general election campaign of a [congressional] candidate." In a plurality opinion, Justice Breyer, joined by Justices O'Connor and Souter, held that, under *Buckley*, the first amendment prohibits the application of this provision to expenditures that the political party makes "independently, without coordination with a candidate," but found it unnecessary to decide whether the provision would be unconstitutional as applied to coordinated expenditures.

In a separate opinion, Justice Kennedy, joined by Chief Justice Rehnquist and Justice Scalia, went further and concluded that the first amendment prohibits the application of this provision even to expenditures that a political party makes "in cooperation, consultation, or concert [with] a candidate." Although the Act characterizes such expenditures as "contributions," which ordinarily would be regulable under *Buckley*, Justice Kennedy argued that "political party spending" in this manner "does not fit within our description of 'contributions' in *Buckley*":

> It makes no sense [to] ask [whether] a party's spending is made "in cooperation, consultation, or concert with" its candidate. [It] would be impractical and imprudent [for] a party to support its own candidates without some form of "cooperation" or "consultation." The party's speech, legitimate on its own behalf,

> cannot be separated from speech on the candidate's behalf without constraining the party in advocating its most essential positions and pursuing its most basic goals. [Party] spending "in cooperation, consultation, or concert with" a candidate [is] indistinguishable in substance from expenditures by the candidate. . . . We held in *Buckley* that the First Amendment does not permit regulations of the latter, and it should not permit this regulation of the former.

In another separate opinion, Justice Thomas, joined by Chief Justice Rehnquist and Justice Scalia, agreed with Justice Kennedy:

> As applied in the specific context of campaign funding by political parties, the anti-corruption rationale [relied on by the Court in *Buckley* to uphold contribution limitations] loses its force. What could it mean for a party to "corrupt" its candidate or to exercise "coercive" influence over him? The very aim of a political party is to influence its candidate's stance on issues and, if the candidate takes [office], his votes. When [a Party] spends large sums of money in support of a candidate who wins, takes office, and then implements the Party's platform, that is not corruption; that is successful advocacy of ideas in the political marketplace and representative government in a party system.

Justice Stevens, joined by Justice Ginsburg, dissented on the ground that "all money spent by a political party to secure the election of its candidate [should] be considered a [regulable] 'contribution,'" whether or not the expenditure is made "in cooperation, consultation, or concert" with the candidate's campaign. Justice Stevens argued that "such limits serve the interest in avoiding both the appearance and the reality of a corrupt political process," they are necessary to "supplement other spending limitations [which] are likewise designed to prevent corruption," and they serve the government's "important interest in leveling the playing field by constraining the cost of federal campaigns."

F. ADDITIONAL PROBLEMS

Page 1452. At the end of section 3 of the Note, add the following:

On the public/private speech distinction, see Gray, Public and Private Speech: Toward a Practice of Pluralistic Convergence in Free-Speech Values, 1 Tex. Wesleyan L. Rev. 1 (1994).

Page 1453. At the end of section 4 of the Note, add the following:

5. *Independent contractors.* Wabaunsee County, Kansas, contracted with respondent for him to be the exclusive hauler of trash for cities in the

county. By its terms, the contract between the county and respondent was automatically renewed annually unless either party terminated it by giving at least sixty days' notice. Respondent was an outspoken critic of the County Board of Commissioners. According to the allegations of respondent's complaint, the Board decided not to renew his contract because of his political opposition to its policies. In Board of County Commissioners, Wabaunsee County, Kansas v. Umbehr, 116 S. Ct. — (1996), the Court held that, like public employees, independent contractors are protected by the first amendment against discharge in retaliation for their speech and that "the *Pickering* balancing test, adjusted to weigh the government's interests as contractor rather than as employer, determines the extent of their protection." See also O'Hare Truck Service, Inc. v. City of Northlake, 116 S. Ct. — (1996) (same result with respect to patronage).

Page 1456. At the end of the paragraph at the bottom of the page discussing Rutan v. Republican Party of Illinois, add the following:

Do *Elrod* and *Branti* apply to independent contractors? O'Hare Truck Service, Inc. v. City of Northlake, 116 S. Ct. — (1996), involved a situation in which the city coordinates towing services and maintains a rotation list of available towing companies. When petitioner refused to make a political contribution to the Mayor's reelection campaign, he was removed from the rotation list. The Court held that, in such circumstances, the protections of *Elrod* and *Branti* govern. See also Board of County Commissioners, Wabaunsee County, Kansas v. Umbehr, 116 S. Ct. — (1996) (same result with respect to political expression critical of the government).

Page 1466. At the end of *Barnette*, add the following:

Is *Barnette* wrong because reasonable observers would understand that the speech was compelled? Consider Greene, The Pledge of Allegiance Problem, 64 Fordham L. Rev. 451, 473, 482 (1995):

> For an act to be considered expressive, and thus worthy of prima facie protection under the Free Speech Clause, that act must involve (or appear to a reasonable observer to involve) the communication of the speaker's internal mental state, such as her beliefs, attitudes or convictions. [Neither] a law compelling the utterance of the pledge of allegiance nor a law compelling a left turn signal requires the agent to reveal the contents of her mind. . . . [Because] a reasonable observer [would] understand the teacher-led pledge of allegiance, with no opt-out provision, as compelled and thus as not reflective of the beliefs of the [students, there is no violation of the free speech clause].

Page 1472. In section 1, after the citation to Turner Broadcasting System, Inc. v. FCC, add the following:

Denver Area Education Telecommunications Consortium, Inc. v. FCC, 116 S. Ct. — (1996) (considering the constitutionality of several provisions of the Cable Television Consumer Protection and Competition Act of 1992 concerning the broadcasting of "indecent" programming on public access and leased access channels);

Page 1525. At the end of section 1 of the Note, add the following:

Is the Court's content-based/content-neutral analysis unhelpful in cases like *Turner*? Consider Bhagwat, Of Markets and Media: The First Amendment, the New Mass Media, and the Political Components of Culture, 74 N. Car. L. Rev. 141, 176 (1995):

> [T]he Court's basic [content-based/content-neutral] analysis [has] performed relatively well in defending individual speakers—generally dissidents with unpopular views—from direct censorship by the government. [That analysis assumes] an atomistic marketplace of speech, speakers, and listeners; and when those assumptions hold, the categories are generally workable. With respect to regulation of the modern mass media, however, where those assumptions assuredly do not hold, the Court's categories tend to collapse, and its [analysis] fails. What is needed [is] a rethinking [of] the underlying doctrine, based on a more realistic model of mass media markets. [S]uch a reappraisal must take into account [both] the role of the mass media in today's society, including its power to shape preferences and discourse through a process of socialization, [and] the danger that the government will seek, through regulation of the media, to take control of that process itself. . . .

Page 1526. Before section 5 of the Note, add the following:

4a. *Regulation of cable: another look.* In Denver Area Educational Telecommunications Consortium, Inc. v. FCC, supra section VII-D-5, this Supplement, the Court considered the constitutionality of several provisions of the Cable Television Consumer Protection and Competition Act of 1992 regulating public access and leased access chanels. In a plurality opinion, Justice Breyer, joined by Justices Stevens, O'Connor, and Souter, maintained that, in light of "the changes taking place in the law, the technology, and the industrial structure related to telecommunications," the Court should adopt a narrow, highly contextual, and fact-specific approach, rather than articulate hard-and-fast rules or import into this new and complex area doctrines developed in other areas of first amendment jurisprudence. Is this a wise approach? Consider the following views, expressed in separate opinions in this case:

a. Justice Souter:

All of the relevant characteristics of cable are presently in a state of technological and regulatory flux. [In such circumstances], we should be shy about saying the final word today about what will be accepted as reasonable tomorrow. [Not] every nuance of our old standards will necessarily do for the new technology. [Thus], the job of the courts [in this area will be to recognize] established First Amendment interests through a close analysis that constrains [government], without wholly incapacitating [it], maintaining the high value of open communication, measuring the costs of regulation by exact attention to fact, and compiling a pedigree of experience with the changing subject. These are familiar judicial responsibilities in times when we know too little to risk the finality of precision, and attention to them will probably take us through the communications revolution. Maybe the judicial obligation to shoulder these responsibilities can itself be captured by a much older rule, familiar to every doctor of medicine: "First, do no harm."

b. Justice Kennedy, joined by Justice Ginsburg:

The plurality opinion [is] adrift. The opinion [applies] no standard, and by this omission loses sight of existing First Amendment doctrine. When confronted with a threat to free speech in the context of an emerging technology, we ought to have the discipline to analyze the case by reference to existing elaborations of constant First Amendment principles. [Rather] than undertake this task, however, the plurality just declares that, all things considered, [the challenged provision] seems fine. [The] novelty and complexity of the case is a reason to look for help from other areas of our First Amendment jurisprudence, not a license to wander into uncharted areas of the law with no compass other than our own opinions about good policy. [Justice] Souter recommends to the Court the precept, "First, do no harm." The question, though, is whether the harm is in sustaining the law or striking it down. If the plurality is concerned about technology's direction, it ought to begin by allowing speech, not suppressing it.

c. Justice Thomas, joined by Chief Justice Rehnquist and Justice Scalia:

For many years, we have failed to articulate how and to what extent the First Amendment protects cable operators, programmers, and viewers from state and federal regulation. I think it is time we did so, and I cannot go along with the plurality's assiduous attempts to avoid addressing that issue openly. [Our] First Amendment distinctions between media, dubious from their infancy, placed cable in a doctrinal wasteland in which regulators and cable operators alike could not be sure whether cable was entitled to the substantial First Amendment protections afforded the print media or was subject to the more onerous obligations shouldered by the broadcast media. [In] *Turner*, by adopting much of the print paradigm, and by rejecting *Red Lion*, we adopted with it a considerable body of precedent that governs the respective First Amendment rights of competing speakers. In *Red Lion,* we [legitimized] consideration of the public interest and emphasized the rights of viewers, at least in the abstract. Under that view, "[i]t is the right of the viewers and listeners, not the right of broadcasters, which is paramount." After *Turner,* however, that view can no longer be given any credence in the cable context. It is the operator's right that is preeminent.

4b. *Cable operators v. cable programmers.* In the Cable Act of 1984, Congress authorized local governments to require cable operators to set aside a certain number of channels for "public, educational, or governmental use." The 1984 Act expressly prohibited cable operators from exercising any editorial control over the content of programs broadcast on such "public-access" channels. In the Cable Television Consumer Protection and Competition Act of 1992, Congress altered this scheme and authorized cable operators to restrict on public-access channels programming that depicts or describes "sexual activities or organs in a patently offensive manner." In Denver Area Educational Telecommunications Consortium, Inc. v. FCC, supra section VII-D-5, this Supplement, the Court invalidated this provision. Consider the argument of Justice Thomas, joined by Chief Justice Rehnquist and Justice Scalia, in dissent:

> [Programmers have no first amendment] right to transmit over an operator's cable system. [Accordingly], when there is a conflict, a programmer's asserted right to transmit over an operator's cable system must give way to the operator's editorial discretion. [Citing *Tornillo].* Drawing an analogy to the print media, [the] author of a book [has] no right to have the book sold in a particular bookstore without the store owner's consent. [Thus], the proper question [posed by this regulation is not whether section 10(c) violates the] free speech rights [of programmers because it authorizes operators to restrict indecent expression, but whether the] public access requirements [are] improper restrictions on the operators' free speech rights. [This being so, the programmers cannot] reasonably assert that the Court should strictly scrutinize [section 10(c)] in a way that maximizes their ability to speak [and], by necessity, minimizes the operators' discretion.

Page 1528. After example (c) on the first line of the page, add the following:

In American Civil Liberties Union v. Reno, 1996 U.S. Dist. LEXIS 7919 (E.D. Pa. 1996), the Court of Appeals invalidated as unconstitutionally vague and overbroad the 1996 Communications Decency Act, which prohibited any person from sending over the Internet in a way that would be available to a person under eighteen years of age any "indecent" material, which was defined in the Act as any material that, "in context, depicts or describes, in terms patently offensive as measured by contemporary community standards, sexual or excretory activities or organs." Judge Dalzell explained:

The Internet is a far more speech-enhancing medium than print, the village green, or the mails. [Some] of the dialogue on the Internet surely tests the limits of conventional discourse. Speech on the Internet can be unfiltered, unpolished, and unconventional, [even] "indecent" in many communities. But we should expect such speech to occur in a medium in which citizens from all walks of life have a voice. We should also protect the autonomy that such a medium confers to ordinary people as well as media magnates. [The] Government's permissible supervision of Internet context stops at the traditional line of unprotected speech. [As] the most participatory form of mass speech yet developed, the Internet deserves the highest protection from government intrusion.

Page 1528. At the end of section c. of the Note, add the following:

7. *The liability of cable and on-line carriers for the speech of users.* In what circumstances, if any, should cable or on-line carriers be liable for the libelous, obscene, or otherwise actionable speech they carry? Consider the liability of (a) a store that sells typewriters for the messages typed by purchasers; (b) a telephone company for the speech of callers; (c) a bookstore for the contents of the books it sells; (d) a news vendor for the contents of the newspapers it sells; (e) a newspaper or magazine for the statements made by guest columnists; (f) a cable operator for the programs it carries; and (g) a computer network, such as CompuServe, for the messages it transmits. Should the standards of liability differ across these different situations? Should it matter whether the defendant exercises "editorial" control? Should the defendants in all or some of these cases be liable only "if they have actual notice that the speech has previously been adjudicated illegal or unprotected"? Myerson, Authors, Editors, and Uncommon Carriers: Identifying the "Speaker" Within the New Media, 71 Notre Dame L. Rev. 79, 122 (1995).

Chapter Eight

The Constitution and Religion

A. INTRODUCTION: HISTORICAL AND ANALYTICAL OVERVIEW

Page 1539. Add the following as Note 3a.

3a. *A revisionist defense of originalist approaches.* Consider this comment on *Everson*: "We survivors of this history, Black suggests, adopted the Establishment Clause to commemorate, rather than repeat, it. [Black] is arguing that liberal constitutionalism is a rationale for excluding the promotion of certain historically troubling goals from the public agenda on straightfoward Lincolnian grounds—national unity and a commitment not to repeat the past." Meister, Sojourners and Survivors: Two Logics of Constitutional Protection, 9 Studies in American Pol. Development 229, 276 (1995). Might exclusion of those goals contribute to national disunity instead? To what extent do current controversies implicate a concern not to repeat the past? See Chief Justice Burger's observations in *Lynch v. Donnelly* and Justice Powell's, quoted in *Mueller v. Allen.*

B. THE ESTABLISHMENT CLAUSE

Page 1567. At the end of Note 2, add the following:

Consider this defense of religious liberty founded on the principle of "equal regard": "[One's] status as a member of our political community ought not to depend in any way upon one's religious beliefs. [The] government is obliged to treat the deep religious commitments of members of minority religious faiths with the same regard as it treats the deep commitments of other members of the society. [Government] policy must be justified by public reason, by secular reasons recognizable by—and in principle, endorsable by—any person committed to living in a pluralist society governed by the precepts of equal regard. [Government] must not act so as to divide the community along lines of religious affiliation." Eisgruber

& Sager, Unthinking Religious Freedom, 74 Tex. L. Rev. 577, 600-601 (1996). In response to the criticism that this "amounts to a 'secular establishment,'" Eisgruber and Sager reply, this "would overlook the distinction between a secular constitution and a secular faith. One can reject the idea that the civil government should presuppose the truth of some religious faith without thereby rejecting religion. Many religious views [are] consistent with the idea that constitutional principles should be justified on secular grounds." Id. at 604. Does this approach offer equal regard to religious views that are inconsistent with that idea?

Chapter Ten

The Constitution, Baselines, and the Problem of Private Power

D. CONSTITUTIONALLY REQUIRED DEPARTURES FROM NEUTRALITY? THE PUBLIC FUNCTION DOCTRINE

Page 1756. Before section 2 of the Note, add the following:

g. What implications does *Jackson* hold for the treatment of political parties as state actors? The Court debated this issue in Morse v. Republican Party of Virginia, 116 S. Ct. 1186 (1996). The case presented the court with a question of statutory construction—whether the Virginia Republican Party was obligated under the 1965 Voting Rights Act to obtain preclearance before changing the qualifications for participation in a state nominating convention. In the course of answering this question (in the affirmative), the Court had occasion to distinguish its prior state action precedent:

> In [*Jackson*] and [*Flagg Brothers*] this Court concluded that the defendants were not acting under authority explicitly or implicitly delegated by the State when they carried out the challenged actions. In this case, however, . . . the Party acted under the authority conferred by the Virginia election code. It was the Commonwealth of Virginia—indeed *only* Virginia—that had exclusive power to reserve one of the two special ballot provisions for the Party.

Compare Justice Thomas's dissent:

> The Party's selection of a candidate at a convention does not satisfy [the exclusive public function] test. [We] have carefully distinguished the "conduct" of an election by the State from the exercise of private political rights within that State-created framework. Providing an orderly and fair process for the selection of public officers is a classic exclusive state function. . . .
>
> [By] contrast, convening the members of a political association in order to select the person who can best represent and advance the group's goals is not, and historically has never been, the province of the State—much less its exclusive province.

To be sure, the Party takes advantage of favorable State law when it certifies its candidate for automatic placement on the ballot. Nevertheless, according to our state action cases, that is no basis for treating the Party as the State. The State's conferral of benefits upon an entity—even so great a benefit as monopoly status—is insufficient to convent the entity into a State actor. *See* [*Jackson*].